questions by
Judith Dillingham
Christa Chapman
Laurie Kagan

created and designed by
Miguel Kagan

illustrated by
Celso Rodriguez

Kagan

Kagan Publishing
981 Calle Amanecer
San Clemente, CA 92673-2008
1 (800) 933-2667
www.KaganOnline.com

ISBN: 978-1-879097-49-0

Table of ? Contents

I had six
honest serving men
They taught me all I knew:
Their names were Where
and What and When
and Why and How and
Who.

— Rudyard Kipling

Introduction

In your hands you hold a powerful book. It is a member of a series of transformative blackline activity books. Between the covers, you will find questions, questions, and more questions! But these are no ordinary questions. These are the important kind—higher-level thinking questions—the kind that stretch your students' minds; the kind that release your students' natural curiosity about the world; the kind that rack your students' brains; the kind that instill in your students a sense of wonderment about your curriculum.

But we are getting a bit ahead of ourselves. Let's start from the beginning. Since this is a book of questions, it seems only appropriate for this introduction to pose a few questions—about the book and its underlying educational philosophy. So Mr. Kipling's Six Honest Serving Men, if you will, please lead the way:

What?
What are higher-level thinking questions?

This is a loaded question (as should be all good questions). Using our analytic thinking skills, let's break this question down into two smaller questions: 1) What is higher-level thinking? and 2) What are questions? When we understand the types of thinking skills and the types of questions, we can combine the best of both worlds, crafting beautiful questions to generate the range of higher-level thinking in our students!

Types of Thinking

There are many different types of thinking. Some types of thinking include:

- applying
- associating
- comparing
- contrasting
- defining
- elaborating
- empathizing
- experimenting
- generalizing
- investigatin
- making analogies
- planning
- prioritizing
- recalling
- reflecting
- reversing
- sequencing
- summarizing
- synthesizing
- assessing
- augmenting
- connecting
- decision-making
- drawing conclusions
- eliminating
- evaluating
- explaining
- inferring consequences
- inventing
- memorizing
- predicting
- problem-solving
- reducing
- relating
- role-taking
- substituting
- symbolizing
- understanding
- thinking about thinking (metacognition)

This is quite a formidable list. It's nowhere near complete. Thinking is a big, multifaceted phenomenon. Perhaps the most widely recognized system for classifying thinking and classroom questions is Benjamin Bloom's Taxonomy of Thinking Skills. Bloom's Taxonomy classifies thinking skills into six hierarchical levels. It begins with the lower levels of thinking skills and moves up to higher-level thinking skills: 1) Knowledge, 2) Comprehension, 3) Application, 4) Analysis, 5) Synthesis, 6) Evaluation. See Bloom's Taxonomy on the following page.

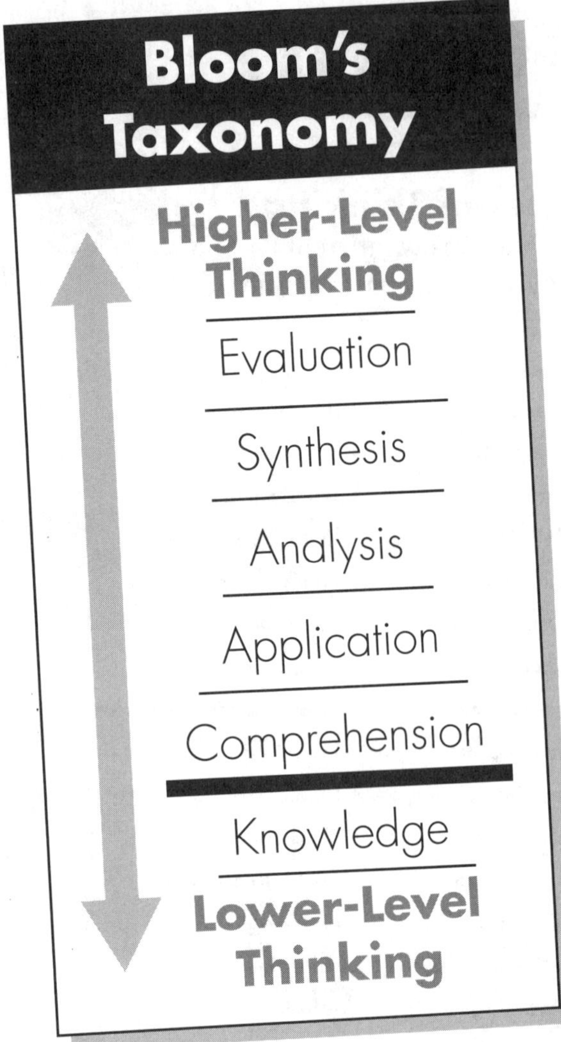

In education, the term "higher-level thinking" often refers to the higher levels of Mr. Bloom's taxonomy. But Bloom's Taxonomy is but one way of organizing and conceptualizing the various types of thinking skills.

There are many ways we can cut the thinking skills pie. We can alternatively view the many different types of thinking skills as, well…many different skills. Some thinking skills may be hierarchical. Some may be interrelated. And some may be relatively independent.

In this book, we take a pragmatic, functional approach. Each type of thinking skill serves a different function. So called "lower-level" thinking skills are very useful for certain purposes. Memorizing and understanding information are invaluable skills that our students will use throughout their lives. But so too are many of the "higher-level" thinking skills on our list. The more facets of students' thinking skills we develop, the better we prepare them for lifelong success.

Because so much classroom learning heretofore has focused on the "lower rungs" of the thinking skills ladder—knowledge and comprehension, or memorization and understanding—in this series of books we have chosen to focus on questions to generate "higher-level" thinking. This book is an attempt to correct the imbalance in the types of thinking skills developed by classroom questions.

Types of Questions

As we ask questions of our students, we further promote cognitive development when we use Fat questions, Low-Consensus questions, and True questions.

Fat Questions vs. Skinny Questions

Skinny questions are questions that require a skinny answer. For example, after reading a poem, we can ask: "Did you like the poem?" Even though this question could be categorized as an Evaluation question—Bloom's highest level of thinking— it can be answered with one monosyllabic word: "Yes" or "No." How much thinking are we actually generating in our students?

We can reframe this question to make it a fat question: "What things did you like about the poem? What things did you dislike?" Notice no short answer will do. Answering this fattened-up question requires more elaboration. These fat questions presuppose not that there is only one thing but things plural that the student liked and things that she did not like. Making things plural is one way to make skinny questions fat. Students stretch their minds to come up with multiple ideas or solutions. Other easy ways to make questions fat is to add "Why or why not?" or "Explain" or "Describe" or "Defend your position" to the end of a question. These additions promote elaboration beyond a skinny answer. Because language and thought are intimately intertwined, questions that require elaborate responses stretch students' thinking: They grapple to articulate their thoughts.

The type of questions we ask impact not just the type of thinking we develop in our students, but also the depth of thought. Fat questions elicit fat responses. Fat responses develop both depth of thinking and range of thinking skills. The questions in this book are designed to elicit fat responses—deep and varied thinking.

High-Consensus Questions vs. Low-Consensus Questions

A high-consensus question is one to which most people would give the same response, usually a right or wrong answer. After learning about sound, we can ask our students: "What is the name of a room specially designed to improve acoustics for the audience?" This is a high-consensus question. The answer (auditorium) is either correct or incorrect.

Compare the previous question with a low-consensus question: "If you were going to build an auditorium, what special design features would you take into consideration?" Notice, to the low-consensus question there is no right or wrong answer. Each person formulates his or her unique response. To answer, students must apply what they learned, use their ingenuity and creativity.

High-consensus questions promote convergent thinking. With high-consensus questions we strive to direct students **what to think**. Low-consensus questions promote divergent thinking, both critical and creative. With low-consensus

questions we strive to develop students' **ability to think**. The questions in this book are low-consensus questions designed to promote independent, critical and creative thought.

True Questions vs. Review Questions

We all know what review questions are. They're the ones in the back of every chapter and unit. Review questions ask students to regurgitate previously stated or learned information. For example, after learning about the rain forest we may ask: "What percent of the world's oxygen does the rain forest produce?" Students can go back a few pages in their books or into their memory banks and pull out the answer. This is great if we are working on memorization skills, but does little to develop "higher-order" thinking skills.

True questions, on the other hand, are meaningful questions—questions to which we do not know the answer. For example: "What might happen if all the world's rain forests were cut down?" This is a hypothetical; we don't know the answer but considering the question forces us to think. We infer some logical consequences based on what we know. The goal of true questions is not a correct answer, but the thinking journey students take to create a meaningful response. True questions are more representative of real life. Seldom is there a black and white answer. In life, we struggle with ambiguity, confounding variables, and uncertain outcomes. There are millions of shades of gray. True questions prepare students to deal with life's uncertainties.

When we ask a review question, we know the answer and are checking to see if the student does also. When we ask a true question, it is truly a question. We don't necessarily know the answer and neither does the student. True questions are

> **Education is not the filling of a pail, but the lighting of a fire.**
>
> — William Butler Yeats

Types of Questions

Skinny ➡ **Fat**
- Short Answer
- Shallow Thinking

- Elaborated Answer
- Deep Thinking

High-Consensus ➡ **Low-Consensus**
- Right or Wrong Answer
- Develops Convergent Thinking
- "What" to Think

- No Single Correct Answer
- Develops Divergent Thinking
- "How" to Think

Review ➡ **True**
- Asker Knows Answer
- Checking for Correctness

- Asker Doesn't Know Answer
- Invitation to Think

often an invitation to think, ponder, speculate, and engage in a questioning process.

We can use true questions in the classroom to make our curriculum more personally meaningful, to promote investigation, and awaken students' sense of awe and wonderment in what we teach. Many questions you will find in this book are true questions designed to make the content provocative, intriguing, and personally relevant.

The box above summarizes the different types of questions. The questions you will find in this book are a move away from skinny, high-consensus, review questions toward fat, low-consensus true questions. As we ask these types of questions in our class, we transform even mundane content into a springboard for higher-level thinking. As we integrate these question gems into our daily lessons, we create powerful learning experiences. ***We do not fill our students' pails with knowledge; we kindle their fires to become lifetime thinkers.***

Why?

Why should I use higher-level thinking questions in my classroom?

As we enter the new millennium, major shifts in our economic structure are changing the ways we work and live. The direction is increasingly toward an information-based, high-tech economy. The sum of our technological information is exploding. We could give you a figure how rapidly information is doubling, but by the time you read this, the number would be outdated! No kidding.

But this is no surprise. This is our daily reality. We see it around us everyday and on the news: cloning, gene manipulation, e-mail, the Internet, Mars rovers, electric cars, hybrids, laser surgery, CD-ROMs, DVDs. All around us we see the wheels of progress turning: New discoveries, new technologies, a new societal knowledge and information base. New jobs are being created today in fields that simply didn't exist yesterday.

How do we best prepare our students for this uncertain future—a future in which the only constant will be change? As we are propelled into a world of ever-increasing change, what is the relative value of teaching students facts versus thinking skills? This point becomes even more salient when we realize that students cannot master everything, and many facts will soon become obsolete. Facts become outdated or irrelevant. Thinking skills are for a lifetime. Increasingly, how we define educational success will be away from the quantity of information mastered. Instead, we will define success as our students' ability to generate questions, apply, synthesize, predict, evaluate, compare, categorize.

If we as a professionals are to proactively respond to these societal shifts, thinking skills will become central to our curriculum. Whether we teach thinking skills directly, or we integrate them into our curriculum, the power to think is the greatest gift we can give our students!

We believe the questions you will find in this book are a step in the direction of preparing students for lifelong success. The goal is to develop independent thinkers who are critical and creative, regardless of the content. We hope the books in this series are more than sets of questions. We provide them as a model approach to questioning in the classroom.

On pages 8 and 9, you will find Questions to Engage Students' Thinking Skills. These pages contain numerous types of thinking and questions designed to engage each thinking skill. As you make your own questions for your students with your own content, use these question starters to help you frame

> # Virtually the only predictable trend is continuing change.
>
> — Dr. Linda Tsantis,
> Creating the Future

your questions to stimulate various facets of your students' thinking skills. Also let your students use these question starters to generate their own higher-level thinking questions about the curriculum.

Who?
Who is this book for?

This book is for you and your students, but mostly for your students. It is designed to help make your job easier. Inside you will find hundreds of ready-to-use reproducible questions. Sometimes in the press for time we opt for what is easy over what is best. These books attempt to make easy what is best. In this treasure chest, you will find hours and hours of timesaving ready-made questions and activities.

Place Higher-Level Thinking In Your Students' Hands

As previously mentioned, this book is even more for your students than for you. As teachers, we ask a tremendous number of questions. Primary teachers ask 3.5 to 6.5 questions per minute! Elementary teachers average 348 questions a day. How many questions would you predict our students ask? Researchers asked this question. What they found was shocking: Typical students ask approximately one question per month.* One question per month!

Although this study may not be representative of your classroom, it does suggest that in general, as teachers we are missing out on a very powerful force—student-generated questions. The capacity to answer higher-level thinking questions is

---

* Myra & David Sadker, "Questioning Skills" in *Classroom Teaching Skills*, 2nd ed. Lexington, MA: D.C. Heath & Co., 1982.

Questions to Engage Students' Thinking Skills

Analyzing
• How could you break down…?
• What components…?
• What qualities/characteristics…?

Applying
• How is _____ an example of…?
• What practical applications…?
• What examples…?
• How could you use…?
• How does this apply to…?
• In your life, how would you apply…?

Assessing
• By what criteria would you assess…?
• What grade would you give…?
• How could you improve…?

Augmenting/Elaborating
• What ideas might you add to…?
• What more can you say about…?

Categorizing/Classifying/Organizing
• How might you classify…?
• If you were going to categorize…?

Comparing/Contrasting
• How would you compare…?
• What similarities…?
• What are the differences between…?
• How is _____ different…?

Connecting/Associating
• What do you already know about…?
• What connections can you make between…?
• What things do you think of when you think of…?

Decision-Making
• How would you decide…?
• If you had to choose between…?

Defining
• How would you define…?
• In your own words, what is…?

Describing/Summarizing
• How could you describe/summarize…?
• If you were a reporter, how would you describe…?

Determining Cause/Effect
• What is the cause of…?
• How does _____ effect _____?
• What impact might…?

Drawing Conclusions/ Inferring Consequences
• What conclusions can you draw from…?
• What would happen if…?
• What would have happened if…?
• If you changed _____, what might happen?

Eliminating
• What part of _____ might you eliminate?
• How could you get rid of…?

Evaluating
• What is your opinion about…?
• Do you prefer…?
• Would you rather…?
• What is your favorite…?
• Do you agree or disagree…?
• What are the positive and negative aspects of…?
• What are the advantages and disadvantages…?
• If you were a judge…?
• On a scale of 1 to 10, how would you rate…?
• What is the most important…?
• Is it better or worse…?

Explaining
• How can you explain…?
• What factors might explain…?

Experimenting

- How could you test…?
- What experiment could you do to…?

Generalizing

- What general rule can…?
- What principle could you apply…?
- What can you say about all…?

Interpreting

- Why is _____ important?
- What is the significance of…?
- What role…?
- What is the moral of…?

Inventing

- What could you invent to…?
- What machine could…?

Investigating

- How could you find out more about…?
- If you wanted to know about…?

Making Analogies

- How is _____ like _____?
- What analogy can you invent for…?

Observing

- What observations did you make about…?
- What changes…?

Patterning

- What patterns can you find…?
- How would you describe the organization of…?

Planning

- What preparations would you…?

Predicting/Hypothesizing

- What would you predict…?
- What is your theory about…?
- If you were going to guess…?

Prioritizing

- What is more important…?
- How might you prioritize…?

Problem-Solving

- How would you approach the problem?
- What are some possible solutions to…?

Reducing/Simplifying

- In a word, how would you describe…?
- How can you simplify…?

Reflecting/Metacognition

- What would you think if…?
- How can you describe what you were thinking when…?

Relating

- How is _____ related to _____?
- What is the relationship between…?
- How does _____ depend on _____?

Reversing/Inversing

- What is the opposite of…?

Role-Taking/Empathizing

- If you were (someone/something else)…?
- How would you feel if…?

Sequencing

- How could you sequence…?
- What steps are involved in…?

Substituting

- What could have been used instead of…?
- What else could you use for…?
- What might you substitute for…?
- What is another way…?

Symbolizing

- How could you draw…?
- What symbol best represents…?

Synthesizing

- How could you combine…?
- What could you put together…?

a wonderful skill we can give our students, as is the skill to solve problems. Arguably more important skills are the ability to find problems to solve and formulate questions to answer. If we look at the great thinkers of the world—the Einsteins, the Edisons, the Freuds— their thinking is marked by a yearning to solve tremendous questions and problems. It is this questioning process that distinguishes those who illuminate and create our world from those who merely accept it.

Make Learning an Interactive Process

Higher-level thinking is not just something that occurs between students' ears! Students benefit from an interactive process. This basic premise underlies the majority of activities you will find in this book.

As students discuss questions and listen to others, they are confronted with differing perspectives and are pushed to articulate their own thinking well beyond the level they could attain on their own. Students too have an enormous capacity to mediate each other's learning. When we heterogeneously group students to work together, we create an environment to move students through their zone of proximal development. We also provide opportunities for tutoring and leadership. Verbal interaction with peers in cooperative groups adds a dimension to questions not available with whole-class questions and answers.

> **Asking a good question requires students to think harder than giving a good answer.**
>
> — Robert Fisher,
> Teaching Children
> to Learn

Reflect on this analogy: If we wanted to teach our students to catch and throw, we could bring in one tennis ball and take turns throwing it to each student and having them throw it back to us. Alternatively, we could bring in twenty balls and have our students form small groups and have them toss the ball back and forth to each other. Picture the two classrooms: One with twenty balls being caught at any one moment, and the other with just one. In which class would students better and more quickly learn to catch and throw?

The same is true with thinking skills. When we make our students more active participants in the learning process, they are given dramatically more opportunities to produce their own thought and to strengthen their own thinking skills. Would you rather have one question being asked and answered at any one moment in your class, or twenty? Small groups mean more questioning and more thinking. Instead of rarely answering a teacher question or rarely generating their own question, asking and answering questions becomes a regular part of your students' day. It is through cooperative interaction that we truly turn our classroom into a higher-level think tank. The associated personal and social benefits are invaluable.

When?
When do I use higher-level thinking questions?

Do I use these questions at the beginning of the lesson, during the lesson, or after? The answer, of course, is all of the above.

Use these questions or your own thinking questions at the beginning of the lesson to provide a motivational set for the lesson. Pique students' interest about the content with some provocative questions: "What would happen if we didn't have gravity?" "Why did Pilgrims get along with some Native Americans, but not others?" "What do you think this book will be about?" Make the content personally relevant by bringing in students' own knowledge, experiences, and feelings about the content: "What do you know about spiders?" "What things do you like about mystery stories?" "How would you feel if explorers invaded your land and killed your family?" "What do you wonder about electricity?"

Use the higher-level thinking questions throughout your lessons. Use the many questions and activities in this book not as a replacement of your curriculum, but as an additional avenue to explore the content and stretch students' thinking skills.

Use the questions after your lesson. Use the higher-level thinking questions, a journal writing activity, or the question starters as an extension activity to your lesson or unit.

Or just use the questions as stand-alone sponge activities for students or teams who have finished their work and need a challenging project to work on.

It doesn't matter when you use them, just use them frequently. As questioning becomes a habitual part of the classroom day, students' fear of asking silly questions is diminished. As the ancient Chinese proverb states, "Those who ask a silly question may seem a fool for five minutes, but those who do not ask remain a fool for life."

> **The important thing is to never stop questioning.**
>
> — Albert Einstein

As teachers, we should make a conscious effort to ensure that a portion of the many questions we ask on a daily basis are those that move our students beyond rote memorization. When we integrate higher-level thinking questions into our daily lessons, we transform our role from transmitters of knowledge to engineers of learning.

Where?
Where should I keep this book?

Keep it close by. Inside there are 16 sets of questions. Pull it out any time you teach these topics or need a quick, easy, fun activity or journal writing topic.

How?
How do I get the most out of this book?

In this book you will find 16 topics arranged alphabetically. For each topic there are reproducible pages for: 1) 16 Question Cards, 2) a Journal Writing activity page, 3) and a Question Starters activity page.

1. Question Cards

The Question Cards are truly the heart of this book. There are numerous ways the Question Cards can be used. After the other activity pages are introduced, you will find a description of a variety of engaging formats to use the Question Cards.

Specific and General Questions

Some of the questions provided in this book series are content-specific and others are content-free. For example, the literature questions in the Literature books are content-specific. Questions for the Great Kapok Tree deal specifically with that literature selection. Some language arts questions in the Language Arts book, on the other hand, are content-free. They are general questions that can be used over and over again with new content. For example, the Book Review questions can be used after reading any book. The Story Structure questions can be used after reading any story. You can tell by glancing at the title of the set and some of the questions whether the set is content-specific or content-free.

A Little Disclaimer

Not all of the "questions" on the Question Cards are actually questions. Some instruct students to do something. For example, "Compare and contrast…" We can also use these directives to develop the various facets of students' thinking skills.

The Power of Think Time

As you and your students use these questions, don't forget about the power of Think Time! There are two different think times. The first is the time between the question and the response. The second is the time between the response and feedback on the response. Think time has been shown to greatly enhance the quality of student thinking. If students are not pausing for either think time, or doing it too briefly, emphasize its importance. Five little seconds of silent think time after the question and five more seconds before feedback are proven, powerful ways to promote higher-level thinking in your class.

Use Your Question Cards for Years

For attractive Question Cards that will last for years, photocopy them on color card-stock paper and laminate them. To save time, have the Materials Monitor from each team pick up one card set, a pair of scissors for the team, and an envelope or rubber band. Each team cuts out their own set of Question Cards. When they are done with the activity, students can place the Question Cards in the envelope and write the name of the set on the envelope or wrap the cards with a rubber band for storage.

Higher-Level Thinking Questions for Intermediate Literature
Kagan Publishing • 1 (800) 933-2667 • www.KaganOnline.com

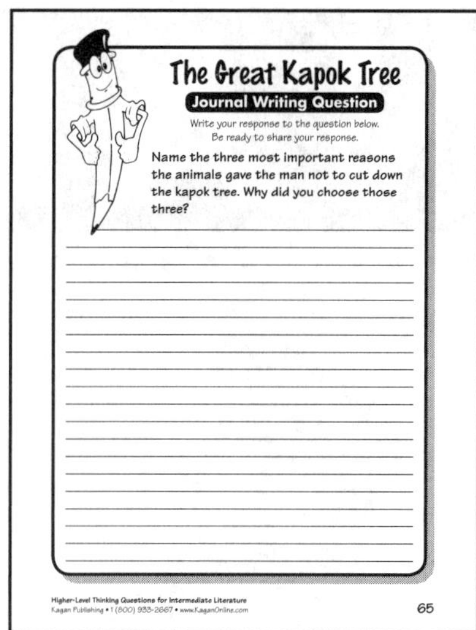

2. Journal Question

The Journal Writing page contains one of the 16 questions as a journal writing prompt. You can substitute any question, or use one of your own. The power of journal writing cannot be overstated. The act of writing takes longer than speaking and thinking. It allows the brain time to make deep connections to the content. Writing requires the writer to present his or her response in a clear, concise language. Writing develops both strong thinking and communication skills.

A helpful activity before journal writing is to have students discuss the question in pairs or in small teams. Students discuss their ideas and what they plan to write. This little prewriting activity ignites ideas for those students who stare blankly at their Journal Writing page. The interpersonal interaction further helps students articulate what they are thinking about the topic and invites students to delve deeper into the topic.

Tell students before they write that they will share their journal entries with a partner or with their team. This motivates many students to improve their entry. Sharing written responses also promotes flexible thinking with open-ended questions, and allows students to hear their peers' responses, ideas and writing styles.

Have students keep a collection of their journal entries in a three-ring binder. This way you can collect them if you wish for assessment or have students go back to reflect on their own learning. If you are using questions across the curriculum, each subject can have its own journal or own section within the binder. Use the provided blackline on the following page for a cover for students' journals or have students design their own.

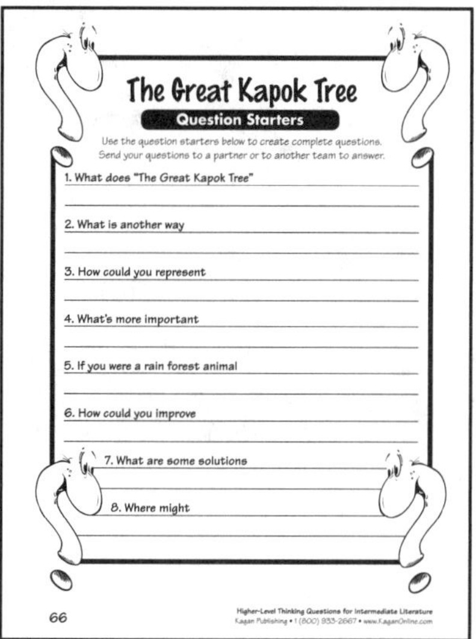

3. Question Starters

The Question Starters activity page is designed to put the questions in the hands of your students. Use these question starters to scaffold your students' ability to write their own thinking questions. This page includes eight question starters to direct students to generate questions across the levels and types of thinking. This Question Starters activity page can be used in a few different ways:

Individual Questions

Have students independently come up with their own questions. When done, they can trade their questions with a partner. On a separate sheet of paper students answer their partners' questions. After answering, partners can share how they answered each other's questions.

JOURNAL

My Best Thinking

____

This Journal Belongs to

Higher-Level Thinking Questions for Intermediate Literature
Kagan Publishing • 1 (800) 933-2667 • www.KaganOnline.com

Pair Questions

Students work in pairs to generate questions to send to another pair. Partners take turns writing each question and also take turns recording each answer. After answering, pairs pair up to share how they answered each other's questions.

Team Questions

Students work in teams to generate questions to send to another team. Teammates take turns writing each question and recording each answer. After answering, teams pair up to share how they answered each other's questions.

Teacher-Led Questions

For young students, lead the whole class in coming up with good higher-level thinking questions.

Teach Your Students About Thinking and Questions

An effective tool to improve students' thinking skills is to teach students about the types of thinking skills and types of questions. Teaching students about the types of thinking skills improves their metacognitive abilities. When students are aware of the types of thinking, they may more effectively plan, monitor, and evaluate their own thinking. When students understand the types of questions and the basics of question construction, they are more likely to create effective higher-level thinking questions. In doing so they develop their own thinking skills and the thinking of classmates as they work to answer each other's questions.

Table of Activities

The Question Cards can be used in a variety of game-like formats to forge students' thinking skills. They can be used for cooperative team and pair work, for whole-class questioning, for independent activities, or at learning centers. On the following pages you will find numerous excellent options to use your Question Cards. As you use the Question Cards in this book, try the different activities listed below to add novelty and variety to the higher-level thinking process.

Activities

team activity #1

Question Commander

Preferably in teams of four, students shuffle their Question Cards and place them in a stack, questions facing down, so that all teammates can easily reach the Question Cards. Give each team a Question Commander set of instructions (blackline provided on following page) to lead them through each question.

Student One becomes the Question Commander for the first question. The Question Commander reads the question aloud to the team, then asks the teammates to think about the question and how they would answer it. After the think time, the Question Commander selects a teammate to answer the question. The Question Commander can spin a spinner or roll a die to select who will answer. After the teammate gives the answer, Question Commander again calls for think time, this time asking the team to think about the answer. After the think time, the Question Commander leads a team discussion in which any teammember can contribute his or her thoughts or ideas to the question, or give praise or reactions to the answer.

When the discussion is over, Student Two becomes the Question Commander for the next question.

Question Commander
Instruction Cards

Question Commander

1. Ask the Question: Question Commander reads the question to the team.
2. Think Time: "Think of your best answer."
3. Answer the Question: The Question Commander selects a teammate to answer the question.
4. Think Time: "Think about how you would answer differently or add to the answer."
5. Team Discussion: As a team, discuss other possible answers or reactions to the answer given.

Question Commander

1. Ask the Question: Question Commander reads the question to the team.
2. Think Time: "Think of your best answer."
3. Answer the Question: The Question Commander selects a teammate to answer the question.
4. Think Time: "Think about how you would answer differently or add to the answer."
5. Team Discussion: As a team, discuss other possible answers or reactions to the answer given.

Question Commander

1. Ask the Question: Question Commander reads the question to the team.
2. Think Time: "Think of your best answer."
3. Answer the Question: The Question Commander selects a teammate to answer the question.
4. Think Time: "Think about how you would answer differently or add to the answer."
5. Team Discussion: As a team, discuss other possible answers or reactions to the answer given.

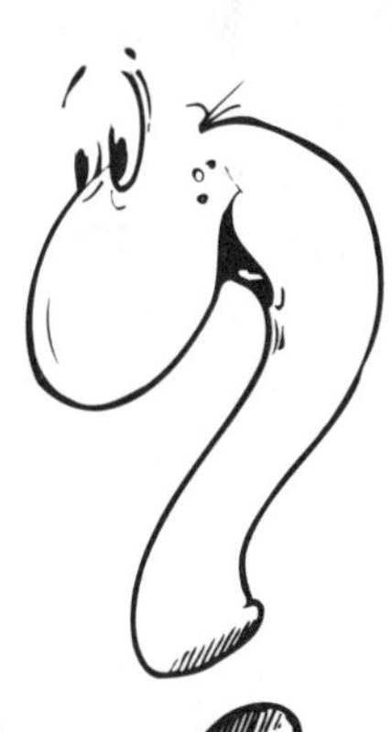

Question Commander

1. Ask the Question: Question Commander reads the question to the team.
2. Think Time: "Think of your best answer."
3. Answer the Question: The Question Commander selects a teammate to answer the question.
4. Think Time: "Think about how you would answer differently or add to the answer."
5. Team Discussion: As a team, discuss other possible answers or reactions to the answer given.

Fan-N-Pick

In a team of four, Student One fans out the question cards, and says, "Pick a card, any card!" Student Two picks a card and reads the question out loud to teammates. After five seconds of think time, Student Three gives his or her answer. After another five seconds of think time, Student Four paraphrases, praises, or adds to the answer given. Students rotate roles for each new round.

Spin-N-Think™

Spin-N-Think spinners are available from Kagan to lead teams through the steps of higher-level thinking. Students spin the Spin-N-Think™ spinner to select a student at each stage of the questioning to: 1) ask the question, 2) answer the question, 3) paraphrase and praise the answer, 4) augment the answer, and 5) discuss the question or answer. The Spin-N-Think™ game makes higher-level thinking more fun, and holds students accountable because they are often called upon, but never know when their number will come up.

Three-Step Interview

After the question is read to the team, students pair up. The first step is an interview in which one student interviews the other about the question. In the second step, students remain with their partner but switch roles: The interviewer becomes the interviewee. In the third step, the pairs come back together and each student in turn presents to the team what their partner shared. Three-Step Interview is strong for individual accountability, active listening, and paraphrasing skills.

Team Discussion

Team Discussion is an easy and informal way of processing the questions: Students read a question and then throw it open for discussion. Team Discussion, however, does not ensure that there is individual accountability or equal participation.

Think-Pair-Square

One student reads a question out loud to teammates. Partners on the same side of the table then pair up to discuss the question and their answers. Then, all four students come together for an open discussion about the question.

Question-Write-RoundRobin

Students take turns asking the team the question. After each question is asked, each student writes his or her ideas on a piece of paper. After students have finished writing, in turn they share their ideas. This format creates strong individual accountability because each student is expected to develop and share an answer for every question.

Mix-Pair-Discuss

Each student gets a different Question Card. For 16 to 32 students, use two sets of questions. In this case, some students may have the same question which is OK. Students get out of their seats and mix around the classroom. They pair up with a partner. One partner reads his or her Question Card and the other answers. Then they switch roles. When done they trade cards and find a new partner. The process is repeated for a predetermined amount of time. The rule is students cannot pair up with the same partner twice. Students may get the same questions twice or more, but each time it is with a new partner. This strategy is a fun, energizing way to ask and answer questions.

Think-Pair-Share

Think-Pair-Share is teacher-directed. The teacher asks the question, then gives students think time. Students then pair up to share their thoughts about the question. After the pair discussion, one student is called on to share with the class what was shared in his or her pair. Think-Pair-Share does not provide as much active participation for students as Think-Pair-Square because only one student is called upon at a time, but is a nice way to do whole-class sharing.

Inside-Outside Circle

Each student gets a Question Card. Half of the students form a circle facing out. The other half forms a circle around the inside circle; each student in the outside circle faces one student in the inside circle. Students in the outside circle ask inside circle students a question. After the inside circle students answer the question, students switch roles questioning and answering. After both have asked and answered a question, they each praise the other's answers and then hold up a hand indicating they are finished. When most students have a hand up, have students trade cards with their partner and rotate to a new partner. To rotate, tell the outside circle to move to the left. This format is a lively and enjoyable way to ask questions and have students listen to the thinking of many classmates.

Question & Answer

This might sound familiar: Instead of giving students the Question Cards, the teacher asks the questions and calls on one student at a time to answer. This traditional format eliminates simultaneous, cooperative interaction, but may be good for introducing younger students to higher-level questions.

Numbered Heads Together

Students number off in their teams so that every student has a number. The teacher asks a question. Students put their "heads together" to discuss the question. The teacher then calls on a number and selects a student with that number to share what his or her team discussed.

RallyRobin

Each pair gets a set of Question Cards. Student A in the pair reads the question out loud to his or her partner. Student B answers. Partners take turns asking and answering each question.

Pair Discussion

Partners take turns asking the question. The pair then discusses the answer together. Unlike RallyRobin, students discuss the answer. Both students contribute to answering and to discussing each other's ideas.

Question-Write-Share-Discuss

One partner reads the Question Card out loud to his or her teammate. Both students write down their ideas. Partners take turns sharing what they wrote. Partners discuss how their ideas are similar and different.

Journal Writing

Students pick one Question Card and make a journal entry or use the question as the prompt for an essay or creative writing. Have students share their writing with a partner or in turn with teammates.

Independent Answers

Students each get their own set of Questions Cards. Pairs or teams can share a set of questions, or the questions can be written on the board or put on the overhead projector. Students work by themselves to answer the questions on a separate sheet of paper. When done, students can compare their answers with a partner, teammates, or the whole class.

Center Ideas

1. Question Card Center

At one center, have the Question Cards and a Spin-N-Think™ spinner, Question Commander instruction card, or Fan-N-Pick instructions. Students lead themselves through the thinking questions. For individual accountability, have each student record their own answer for each question.

2. Journal Writing Center

At a second center, have a Journal Writing activity page for each student. Students can discuss the question with others at their center, then write their own journal entry. After everyone is done writing, students share what they wrote with other students at their center.

3. Question Starters Center

At a third center, have a Question Starters page. Split the students at the center into two groups. Have both groups create thinking questions using the Question Starters activity page. When the groups are done writing their questions, they trade questions with the other group at their center. When done answering each other's questions, two groups pair up to compare their answers.

By the Great Horn Spoon

higher-level thinking questions

**Minds
are like parachutes:
They only function
when open.**

— Thomas R. Dewar

By the Great Horn Spoon
Question Cards

By the Great Horn Spoon

1 What important laws do you think the mining towns needed? What should have been the punishments for breaking these laws?

By the Great Horn Spoon

2 How will Jack's adventures help him when he is an adult? What will Jack's occupation be?

By the Great Horn Spoon

3 What characters in other stories are similar to Jack? In what ways are these characters not like Jack?

By the Great Horn Spoon

4 If you could join Jack in one adventure and change it, which adventure would it be, and how would you change it? Why?

By the Great Horn Spoon
Question Cards

By the Great Horn Spoon

5 When Aunt Arabella arrives, what adventures will Jack definitely not tell her at first? Why? Which adventures will he never tell her?

By the Great Horn Spoon

6 How would Jack's adventures have been different if he had taken a covered wagon instead of a ship to California?

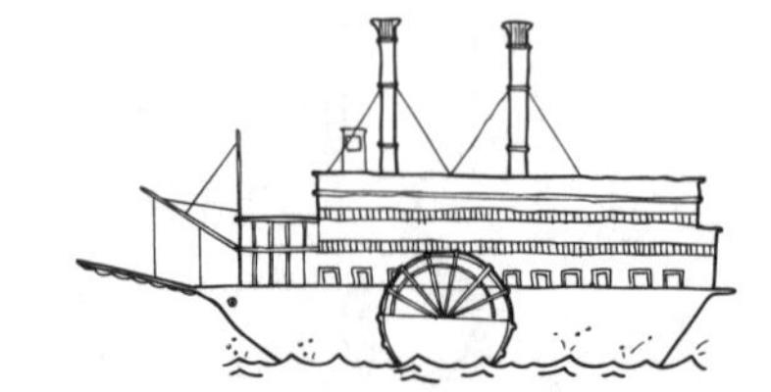

By the Great Horn Spoon

7 What might have happened if Aunt Arabella had gone to California with Jack and Praiseworthy in the beginning?

By the Great Horn Spoon

8 If you were going to make a trip similar to Jack's, what would you want to be sure to pack? Were these things available to Jack?

Higher-Level Thinking Questions for Intermediate Literature
Kagan Publishing • 1 (800) 933-2667 • www.KaganOnline.com

By the Great Horn Spoon
Question Cards

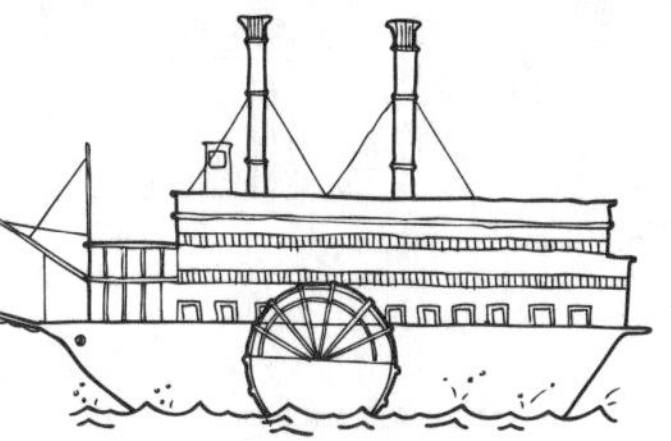

By the Great Horn Spoon

9 How honest have Jack and Praiseworthy been throughout their entire trip? When should or shouldn't they have been more honest?

By the Great Horn Spoon

10 If Jack had been able to see into the future before he left Boston, what decisions might he had made differently?

By the Great Horn Spoon

11 Of all Jack's adventures, which one made the biggest impression on him? Why?

By the Great Horn Spoon

12 After Jack had been in California, how had he changed? What caused these changes? Were they good changes?

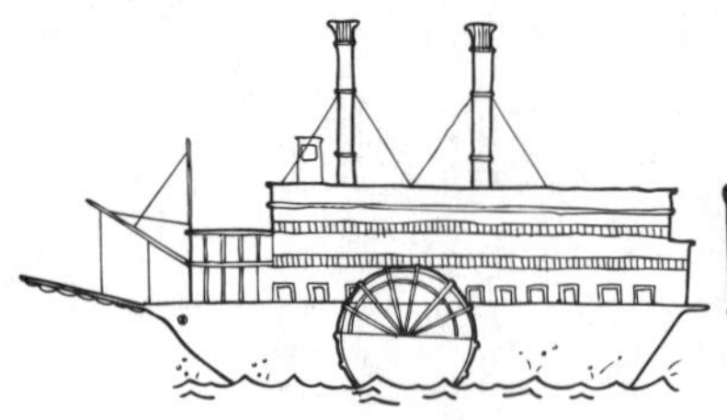

By the Great Horn Spoon
Question Cards

By the Great Horn Spoon

13 If you or your friend had a major problem, how would moving a long distance away help to solve it?

By the Great Horn Spoon

14 The author has used some very unusual names. What do these names tell you about the characters?

By the Great Horn Spoon

15 The ocean voyage was difficult. If the 6:00 news were to interview Jack, what would he tell them about the trip?

By the Great Horn Spoon

16 How were Jack's adventures on the "Lady Wilma" like or unlike his adventures on land?

Higher-Level Thinking Questions for Intermediate Literature
Kagan Publishing • 1 (800) 933-2667 • www.KaganOnline.com

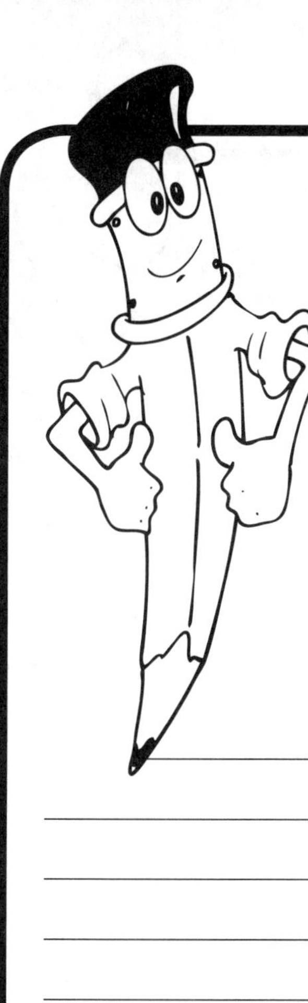

By the Great Horn Spoon

Journal Writing Question

Write your response to the question below.
Be ready to share your response.

The ocean voyage was difficult. If the 6:00 news were to interview Jack, what would he tell them about the trip?

By the Great Horn Spoon

Question Starters

Use the question starters below to create complete questions.
Send your questions to a partner or to another team to answer.

1. If you were Jack

2. What adventure might

3. What is your favorite

4. What would happen if

5. How would you decide

6. What is the relationship

7. What problem

8. What changes

The Cay

higher-level thinking questions

"You can teach a student a lesson for a day; but if you can teach him to learn by creating curiosity, he will continue the learning process as long as he lives."

— Clay P. Bedford

The Cay
Question Cards

The Cay

1 How did Phillip's blindness benefit him?

The Cay

2 How might the relationship between Phillip and Timothy have been different if Phillip had not been blind?

The Cay

3 How did Phillip change while on the island?

The Cay

4 Do you think Phillip's mother really changed, or did Phillip just see her in a new way?

The Cay
Question Cards

The Cay

5 Early in the story the cat was a symbol of evil. What did it symbolize at the end of the story?

The Cay

6 What do you think was the authors purpose for writing this book?

The Cay

7 Who was to blame for Phillip's blindness? Why?

The Cay

8 What career might Phillip be interested in as an adult?

The Cay
Question Cards

The Cay

9 Why did Phillip feel that "holding a hand was like medicine"?

The Cay

10 Describe a time when your opinion of someone changed.

The Cay

11 Choose a new setting for the story and explain how it would change the story.

The Cay

12 Which of your five senses could you live without? Explain your choice.

The Cay
Question Cards

The Cay

13 What did Phillip have in common with the birds?

The Cay

14 What might happen in the sequel to the story?

The Cay

15 How are the hurricane and prejudice alike?

The Cay

16 Create a moral for the story.

The Cay

Journal Writing Question

Write your response to the question below.
Be ready to share your response.

What might happen in the sequel to the story?

The Cay

Question Starters

Use the question starters below to create complete questions.
Send your questions to a partner or to another team to answer.

1. What observations

2. If you were Phillip

3. How can you explain

4. If the story was

5. How would you feel if

6. How could you explain

7. What part of the story

8. What similarities

Charlie and the Chocolate Factory

higher-level thinking questions

"What is the duty of the teacher if not to inspire?

— Bharati Mukherjee

Charlie and the Chocolate Factory
Question Cards

Charlie & the Chocolate Factory

1 You are the author of the story — what would you change? Why?

Charlie & the Chocolate Factory

2 Which parts of the story could really happen? Which parts could not?

Charlie & the Chocolate Factory

3 Pretend it's 30 years later. What changes do you think Charlie would have made in the factory?

Charlie & the Chocolate Factory

4 Which character was your favorite? Why?

Charlie and the Chocolate Factory
Question Cards

Charlie & the Chocolate Factory

5 Make up a new title for the story. What do you like about your title?

Charlie & the Chocolate Factory

6 How might the story have turned out differently if Charlie had not found a winning ticket?

Charlie & the Chocolate Factory

7 Add another contest winner to the story. Give that person a name. What is he or she like? How does he or she get into trouble in the factory?

Charlie & the Chocolate Factory

8 Which character is most like you? Why?

Charlie and the Chocolate Factory
Question Cards

Charlie & the Chocolate Factory

9 If you designed this contest, how would it be different?

Charlie & the Chocolate Factory

10 When Mr. Wonka says, "They'll all come out in the wash." what does he mean?

Charlie & the Chocolate Factory

11 In what other ways could Mr. Wonka have chosen a successor to run the factory?

Charlie & the Chocolate Factory

12 What is Mr. Wonka like? Is he someone you would trust? Why or why not?

Charlie & the Chocolate Factory

13 What might you have done if you were Charlie?

Charlie & the Chocolate Factory

14 What happens to the other children in the end? How have their personalities changed?

Charlie & the Chocolate Factory

15 The grandparents have moved by the factory. What might their new life be like?

Charlie & the Chocolate Factory

16 Did you expect something bad to happen to Charlie? Why or why not?

Charlie and the Chocolate Factory

Journal Writing Question

Write your response to the question below.
Be ready to share your response.

If you designed this contest, how would it be different?

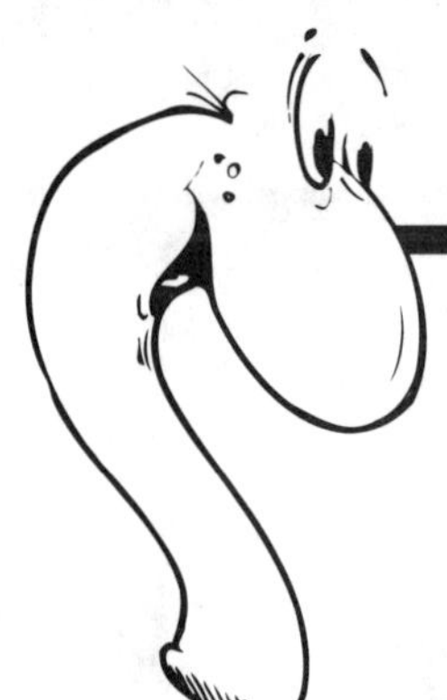

Charlie and the Chocolate Factory

Question Starters

Use the question starters below to create complete questions.
Send your questions to a partner or to another team to answer.

1. What would you predict

2. What if the

3. What is your favorite

4. If the story was

5. Why did the author

6. Will Willy Wonka

7. How important

8. In your life

Charlotte's
Web

higher-level thinking questions

Give a man a fish and you feed him for a day. Teach a man to fish and you feed him for a lifetime.

— Chinese Proverb

Charlotte's Web
Question Cards

1 If you were to make a reading list for Wilber, Charlotte, and Templeton, what books would you recommend? Why?

2 How would the story have been different if Templeton had been a kind, gentle animal?

3 When Charlotte was no longer at the farm, who will give good advice to the animals? What advice will he or she give?

4 If you could have spent one day as one of the animals, which animal would you be and what day would you choose? Explain.

Charlotte's Web
Question Cards

5 What words would you choose for Charlotte to use if she were talking about you?

6 When Fern was an adult, what will she tell her children about Wilber and Charlotte?

7 The egg sac was Charlotte's "masterpiece." What would you create to be your "masterpiece."

8 If the goose, gander, and sheep had known that Charlotte wasn't coming home from the fair, what would they have said to her?

Charlotte's Web
Question Cards

Charlotte's Web

9 Charlotte was important to all the farm animals. What will each of them miss most about her?

Charlotte's Web

10 If you could add one more character to the story, who would it be? What would this character do in the story?

Charlotte's Web

11 If you could hear animals talking, which animals would you like to listen to? What do you think they would talk about?

Charlotte's Web

12 Wilber and Templeton each had their own idea of a "delicious meal." How were they the same or different from your idea of a delicious meal?

Charlotte's Web
Question Cards

Charlotte's Web

13 Wilber was lonely; what farm animals would make the best friends for him?

Charlotte's Web

14 Would Charlotte be a good friend for you? What about her made her a good possibility for a friend?

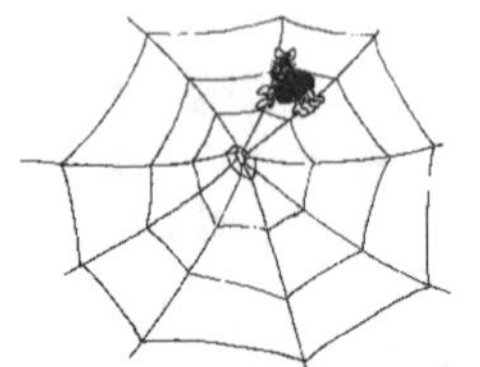

Charlotte's Web

15 Why do you think Templeton acted the way he did? Were the other animals to blame for Templeton's behavior?

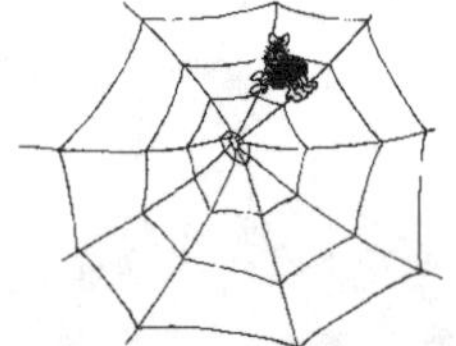

Charlotte's Web

16 If Charlotte had been a "city" spider instead of a "farm" spider, how would her life have been different?

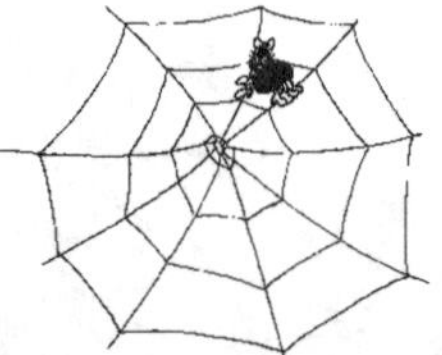

Higher-Level Thinking Questions for Intermediate Literature
Kagan Publishing • 1 (800) 933-2667 • www.KaganOnline.com

Charlotte's Web

Journal Writing Question

Write your response to the question below.
Be ready to share your response.

If Charlotte had been a "city" spider instead of a "farm" spider, how would her life have been different?

Charlotte's Web

Question Starters

Use the question starters below to create complete questions.
Send your questions to a partner or to another team to answer.

1. Do you prefer

2. What was the cause of

3. Why was Templeton

4. How is this book like

5. Which animal

6. If you were Charlotte

7. What would you like

8. If Charlotte was

The Great Kapok Tree

higher-level thinking questions

A teacher who is attempting to teach without inspiring the pupil with a desire to learn is hammering on cold iron.

— Horace Mann

The Great Kapok Tree
Question Cards

The Great Kapok Tree

1 What do you think is a proper solution to the rain forest problem?

The Great Kapok Tree

2 We have U.S. national parks protected from human destruction. Should we have U.N. protected lands? Why or why not?

The Great Kapok Tree

3 Have you ever visited a rain forest? If not, would you like to? Why or why not?

The Great Kapok Tree

4 Did you like the story? Why or why not?

The Great Kapok Tree
Question Cards

The Great Kapok Tree

5 Why *do you* think a forest becomes quiet when humans arrive?

The Great Kapok Tree

6 Give an example of what the following quote means: "...what happens tomorrow depends upon what you do today."

The Great Kapok Tree

7 Name the three most important reasons the animals gave the man not to cut down the kapok tree. Why did you choose those three?

The Great Kapok Tree

8 If you were to become an animal of the rain forest, which one would you be? Why?

Higher-Level Thinking Questions for Intermediate Literature
Kagan Publishing • 1 (800) 933-2667 • www.KaganOnline.com

The Great Kapok Tree
Question Cards

The Great Kapok Tree

9 Who is your favorite animal cartoon character? Would he survive in the rain forest?

The Great Kapok Tree

10 How is man like the bees in the story, depending on each other?

The Great Kapok Tree

11 What new things have you learned or rediscovered about the rain forest?

The Great Kapok Tree

12 Will the man return? Why or why not?

The Great Kapok Tree
Question Cards

The Great Kapok Tree

13 How does cutting down trees in the rain forest affect the food chain?

The Great Kapok Tree

14 Compare man's view of his environment to that of the animals in the story.

The Great Kapok Tree

15 Why did the man drop the ax and walk out?

The Great Kapok Tree

16 The boy asked the man to "look upon them with new eyes." Did he? Why or why not?

Higher-Level Thinking Questions for Intermediate Literature
Kagan Publishing • 1 (800) 933-2667 • www.KaganOnline.com

The Great Kapok Tree

Journal Writing Question

Write your response to the question below.
Be ready to share your response.

Name the three most important reasons the animals gave the man not to cut down the kapok tree. Why did you choose those three?

The Great Kapok Tree

Question Starters

Use the question starters below to create complete questions.
Send your questions to a partner or to another team to answer.

1. What does "The Great Kapok Tree"

2. What is another way

3. How could you represent

4. What's more important

5. If you were a rain forest animal

6. How could you improve

7. What are some solutions

8. Where might

Island of the Blue Dolphins

higher-level thinking questions

Life is amazing, and the teacher had better prepare himself to be a medium for that amazement.

— Edward Blishen

Island of the Blue Dolphins
Question Cards

Island of the Blue Dolphins

1 Do you think the Russians had the right to hunt around the island? Why or why not?

Island of the Blue Dolphins

2 How are Karana and Captain Orlov alike?

Island of the Blue Dolphins

3 Which of your personality traits would be most helpful, if you were in Karana's situation?

Island of the Blue Dolphins

4 Would you have jumped overboard like Karana did? Why or why not?

Island of the Blue Dolphins
Question Cards

Island of the Blue Dolphins

5 What might Ramo have been thinking as he saw the ship leaving the island?

Island of the Blue Dolphins

6 What do you think was Karana's greatest struggle?

Island of the Blue Dolphins

7 How might the island best be used after Karana's rescue?

Island of the Blue Dolphins

8 How do you think Karana really felt about being rescued?

Higher-Level Thinking Questions for Intermediate Literature
Kagan Publishing • 1 (800) 933-2667 • www.KaganOnline.com

Island of the Blue Dolphins
Question Cards

Island of the Blue Dolphins

9 What personality traits enabled Karana to survive on the island for so long?

Island of the Blue Dolphins

10 What three personal items would you want with you on a deserted island?

Island of the Blue Dolphins

11 Why does Karana change her opinion about killing animals?

Island of the Blue Dolphins

12 What might happen to Karana at the mission?

Island of the Blue Dolphins
Question Cards

Island of the Blue Dolphins

13 How did Rontu help Karana?

Island of the Blue Dolphins

14 Which character are you most like? Explain your choice.

Island of the Blue Dolphins

15 If you could mail Karana one book, which book would you send her and why?

Island of the Blue Dolphins

16 Is the story more about life or death? Explain your reasoning.

Higher-Level Thinking Questions for Intermediate Literature
Kagan Publishing • 1 (800) 933-2667 • www.KaganOnline.com

Island of the Blue Dolphins
Journal Writing Question
Write your response to the question below.
Be ready to share your response.
What might happen to Karana at the mission?

Island of the Blue Dolphins
Question Starters

Use the question starters below to create complete questions.
Send your questions to a partner or to another team to answer.

1. What symbol best represents

2. If you were Karana

3. What problems

4. What is the relationship

5. Why did the author

6. How does the setting

7. What conflict

8. How would you describe

Higher-Level Thinking Questions for Intermediate Literature
Kagan Publishing • 1 (800) 933-2667 • www.KaganOnline.com

James and the Giant Peach

higher-level thinking questions

Think for yourselves and let others enjoy the right to do the same.

— Voltaire

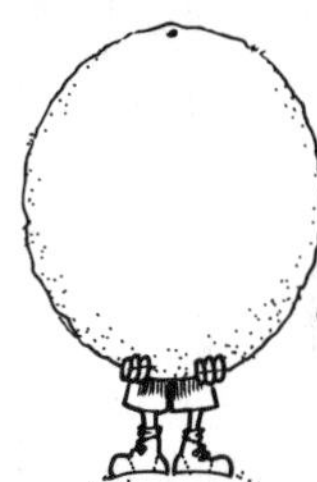

James and the Giant Peach
Question Cards

James and the Giant Peach

1 If you could only take one suitcase to your new home, what would you pack and why?

James and the Giant Peach

2 Would you ever become friends with someone different from yourself? Why or why not?

James and the Giant Peach

3 Which insect was your favorite? Why?

James and the Giant Peach

4 Which of the insects do you think was treated unfairly? Give specifics.

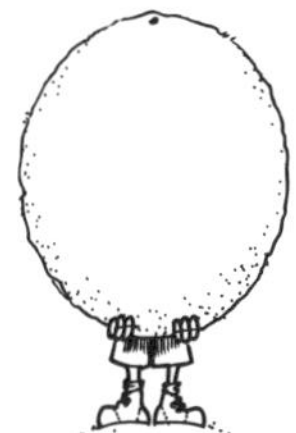

James and the Giant Peach
Question Cards

James and the Giant Peach

5 What would Centipede be like if he was human?

James and the Giant Peach

6 What would you do if a giant peach grew in your yard?

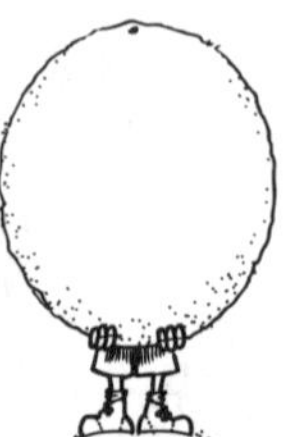

James and the Giant Peach

7 Would you take magic green crystals from a stranger? Why or why not?

James and the Giant Peach

8 Describe James 20 years after arriving in New York City.

Higher-Level Thinking Questions for Intermediate Literature
Kagan Publishing • 1 (800) 933-2667 • www.KaganOnline.com

James and the Giant Peach
Question Cards

James and the Giant Peach

9 How would the story be different if James and his peach had landed in your neighborhood?

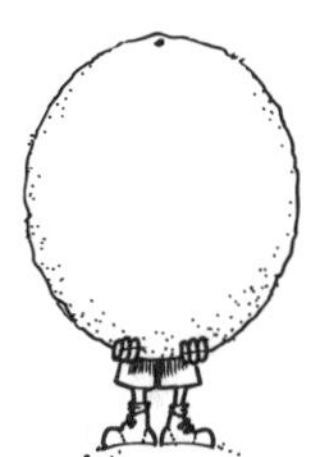

James and the Giant Peach

10 Tell about a new insect that will join James and his friends.

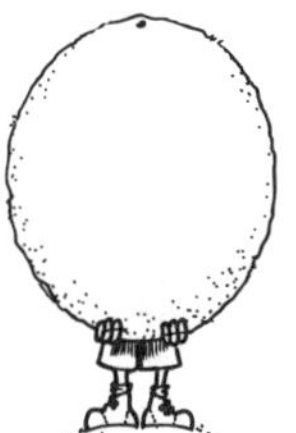

James and the Giant Peach

11 How would the story be different if the main character was a girl?

James and the Giant Peach

12 Which insect is most like you? Why?

James and the Giant Peach
Question Cards

13 What will happen in part two?

14 Why *do you think* the little man gave the crystals to James?

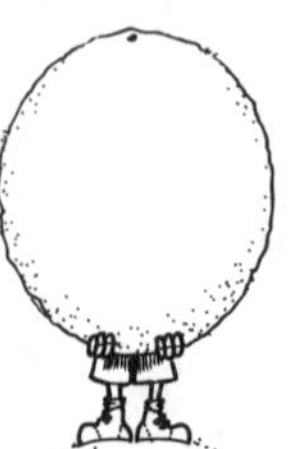

15 What might have happened if James had eaten the magic crystals?

16 If you could ask James anything what would you ask?

Higher-Level Thinking Questions for Intermediate Literature
Kagan Publishing • 1 (800) 933-2667 • www.KaganOnline.com

James and the Giant Peach
Journal Writing Question
Write your response to the question below.
Be ready to share your response.
Tell about a new insect that will join James and his friends.

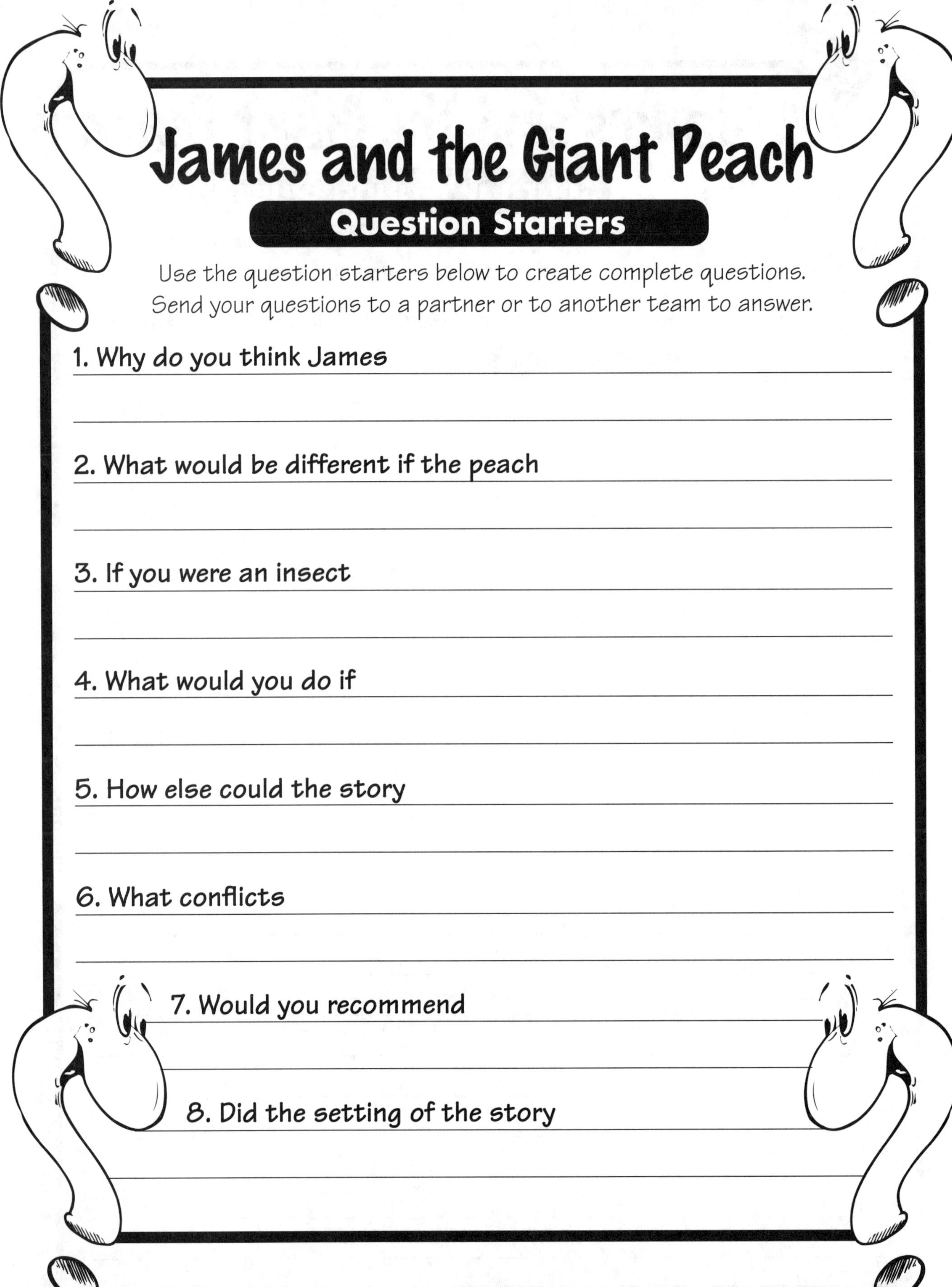

James and the Giant Peach

Question Starters

Use the question starters below to create complete questions.
Send your questions to a partner or to another team to answer.

1. Why do you think James

2. What would be different if the peach

3. If you were an insect

4. What would you do if

5. How else could the story

6. What conflicts

7. Would you recommend

8. Did the setting of the story

Johnny Tremain

higher-level thinking questions

The mediocre teacher tells. The good teacher explains. The superior teacher demonstrates. The great teacher inspires.

— William Arthur Ward

Johnny Tremain
Question Cards

Johnny Tremain

1 Johnny Tremain What might have happened to Johnny if Rab and the Lornes had not taken Johnny in?

Johnny Tremain

2 What good might come as a result of Rab's death? What causes or situations are worth the death of a friend?

Johnny Tremain

3 Johnny will be 22 years old when the Revolutionary War ends. What do you predict for his future?

Johnny Tremain

4 What evidence supports Johnny's statement, "A boy in time of peace, a man in time of war?"

<table>
<tr>
<td>

Johnny Tremain

5 Which historical character from this story would you like to interview? What questions would you ask him?

</td>
<td>

Johnny Tremain

6 If you could change one thing about Johnny's personality, what would it be? Why would you want to make this change?

</td>
</tr>
<tr>
<td>

Johnny Tremain

7 "Loyalist" was not a complimentary term in this story. When should or shouldn't one be loyal? How important is "loyalty"?

</td>
<td>

Johnny Tremain

8 If the Laphams had lived in Concord or Lexington, how would Johnny's contribution to the Revolutionary War have been different?

</td>
</tr>
</table>

Johnny Tremain
Question Cards

Johnny Tremain

9 What contributions did Johnny make to the Revolutionary War? How valuable were these contributions?

Johnny Tremain

10 Which decision of Johnny's made the most difference in his life? What were the results of this decision?

Johnny Tremain

11 What will Johnny tell his children about the Revolutionary War? What will he leave out?

Johnny Tremain

12 Why was spying considered a good thing to do? Would you want to be a spy? Why or why not?

Johnny Tremain
Question Cards

Johnny Tremain

13 Why did Johnny have so much power in the Lapham household at the beginning of the story?

Johnny Tremain

14 What was the most important single event in Johnny's life? Explain.

Johnny Tremain

15 Who was the person with the most longlasting effect on Johnny? Why was this person so powerful?

Johnny Tremain

16 How important were these women to Johnny: Mrs. Lapham, Cilla, Lavinia Lyte, and Johnny's mother? Rank them in order of their importance. Explain.

Higher-Level Thinking Questions for Intermediate Literature
Kagan Publishing • 1 (800) 933-2667 • www.KaganOnline.com

Johnny Tremain

Journal Writing Question

Write your response to the question below.
Be ready to share your response.

What will Johnny tell his children about the Revolutionary War? What will he leave out?

Johnny Tremain

Question Starters

Use the question starters below to create complete questions.
Send your questions to a partner or to another team to answer.

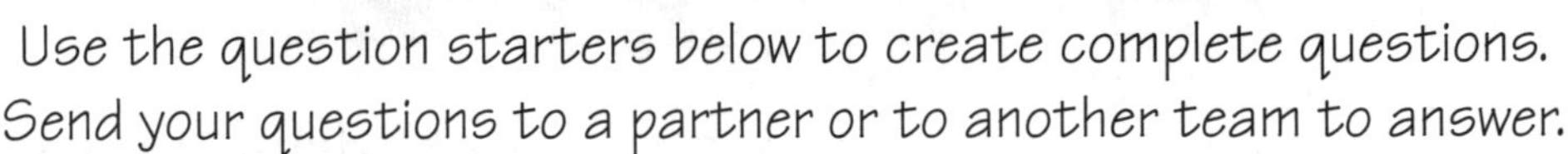

1. How could you compare war

2. Why would Johnny

3. Which character

4. What events

5. How do you feel about

6. What would be different if

7. If you had to choose

8. What is the relationship between

Higher-Level Thinking Questions for Intermediate Literature
Kagan Publishing • 1 (800) 933-2667 • www.KaganOnline.com

Little House on the Prairie

higher-level thinking questions

Judge of a man
by his questions
rather than by his
answers.

— Voltaire

Little House on the Prairie
Question Cards

Little House on the Prairie

1 If you were in the story, how would you have prepared to travel west?

Little House on the Prairie

2 How are you like or unlike Laura Ingalls Wilder?

Little House on the Prairie

3 Change the story so Laura has an older brother instead of her sister Mary. Describe how one event would be different.

Little House on the Prairie

4 Which three modern-day conveniences might have been most useful to the Ingalls family?

Little House on the Prairie
Question Cards

5 Use information from the story to list things you know about Laura's mother.

6 How are Laura and Mary different?

7 Create an adventure in which Laura runs away from home for two days.

8 Step back into that time period. What would be the hardest thing for you about life on the prairie?

Little House on the Prairie
Question Cards

Little House on the Prairie

9 What three things would you like about living in that time period?

Little House on the Prairie

10 Compare the Ingallses' life in Indian country with your life today.

Little House on the Prairie

11 What if Laura had been a boy? Tell what would have been different.

Little House on the Prairie

12 Did any of the characters change during the story? How?

Little House on the Prairie
Question Cards

13 Tell what might have happened if you had been Laura.

14 Use five words to describe Laura.

15 Suppose Laura could have one wish. What might she have wished for? How would that have changed the story?

16 Decide which character you would most like to be. Give your reasons.

Higher-Level Thinking Questions for Intermediate Literature
Kagan Publishing • 1 (800) 933-2667 • www.KaganOnline.com

Little House on the Prairie
Journal Writing Question
Write your response to the question below.
Be ready to share your response.
Compare the Ingallses' life in Indian country with your life today.

Little House on the Prairie

Question Starters

Use the question starters below to create complete questions.
Send your questions to a partner or to another team to answer.

1. What would it be like

2. How should Laura

3. How could you draw

4. What is the importance of

5. What general statement

6. What is your opinion about

7. What role did

8. What conclusion can you draw

Higher-Level Thinking Questions for Intermediate Literature
Kagan Publishing • 1 (800) 933-2667 • www.KaganOnline.com

Lon Po Po

higher-level thinking questions

In teaching it is
the method and not
the content that is the
message...
the drawing out,
not the pumping in.

— Ashley Montague

Lon Po Po
Question Cards

Lon Po Po

1 How would the story have been different if instead of a wolf, there was a leopard? (Leopards can climb trees.)

Lon Po Po

2 When adults leave children, what kind of advice do they give? Explain.

Lon Po Po

3 If the children's father had been in the story, how would the story have been different?

Lon Po Po

4 What other things could the wolf have been tempted with besides ginkgo nuts?

Lon Po Po
Question Cards

Lon Po Po

5 In what other stories have you met a wolf? How were the wolves alike/different?

Lon Po Po

6 How would the story have been different if there had only been one child instead of three children? Explain.

Lon Po Po

7 What might the wolf have done if the children hadn't let him in? Explain.

Lon Po Po

8 How important is their grandmother to the children?

Lon Po Po
Question Cards

Lon Po Po

9 If you were going to disguise yourself as an animal, which animal would you choose and how would your disguise look?

Lon Po Po

10 If Po Po had said she was going to weave a basket and make shoes, why would these have been valuable to the children?

Lon Po Po

11 What other ways besides climbing the ginkgo tree could the children have escaped from the wolf?

Lon Po Po

12 When their mother returned, what did the children tell her about their adventures? What did they leave out?

Lon Po Po
Question Cards

Lon Po Po

13 What questions might the children have asked the wolf to find out if he really were their grandmother?

Lon Po Po

14 What could the mother have done for the grandmother's birthday instead of visiting her?

Lon Po Po

15 Under what circumstances might it be all right to leave children alone? Explain your answer.

Lon Po Po

16 What other reasons could the wolf have given for his low voice, his claws and his tail?

Higher-Level Thinking Questions for Intermediate Literature
Kagan Publishing • 1 (800) 933-2667 • www.KaganOnline.com

Lon Po Po

Journal Writing Question

Write your response to the question below.
Be ready to share your response.

What questions might the children have asked the wolf to find out if he really were their grandmother?

Lon Po Po

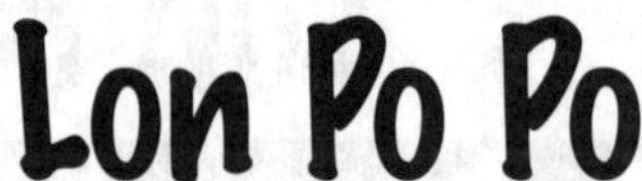

Question Starters

Use the question starters below to create complete questions.
Send your questions to a partner or to another team to answer.

1. In your own experience,

2. What do you know about

3. On a scale of 1 to 5

4. How is this story

5. Would you prefer

6. How could you explain

7. In your

8. If you were the wolf

Higher-Level Thinking Questions for Intermediate Literature
Kagan Publishing • 1 (800) 933-2667 • www.KaganOnline.com

Maniac Magee

higher-level thinking questions

All truly wise thoughts have been thought already thousands of times; but to make them truly ours, we must think them over again honestly, till they take root in our personal experience.

— Johann Wolfgang von Goethe

Maniac Magee
Question Cards

Maniac Magee

1 What could you say to a producer to convince him to make Maniac Magee into a TV program?

Maniac Magee

2 If Maniac had never met Grayson, what difference would it have made in each of their lives? Who gained the most from their friendship?

Maniac Magee

3 When Maniac returns, what will Amanda tell her friends about him?

Maniac Magee

4 If you were to create pictorial symbols for Maniac, Amanda, and Grayson, what would they be?

Maniac Magee
Question Cards

Maniac Magee

5 What events could have occurred during the "lost year"?

Maniac Magee

6 What events or characters in the story have been exaggerated? What could the "real facts" have been?

Maniac Magee

7 Of all Maniac's friends, which one is going to make the most lasting difference in his life? Why?

Maniac Magee

8 How does Maniac deal with basic differences: black/white; young/old; boy/girl?

Higher-Level Thinking Questions for Intermediate Literature
Kagan Publishing • 1 (800) 933-2667 • www.KaganOnline.com

Maniac Magee
Question Cards

Maniac Magee

9 What person or situation do you think Maniac feared the most? Why? Would you have reacted to fear as he did?

Maniac Magee

10 What qualities does Maniac have that make him a good possibility for a friend?

Maniac Magee

11 If you could change one thing about Maniac, what would it be? Why? What would this change do to the story?

Maniac Magee

12 Create another jump rope rhyme about Maniac.

Maniac Magee
Question Cards

13 What events in Maniac's life might have been different had he not been a runner?

14 What other nicknames can you think of for Maniac? Why would these nicknames fit him?

15 If Maniac were to describe himself, what words would he use? What words would Amanda use?

16 If you were assigned to rewrite one chapter in the book, which one would you choose? What would you alter or add? Why?

Higher-Level Thinking Questions for Intermediate Literature
Kagan Publishing • 1 (800) 933-2667 • www.KaganOnline.com

Maniac Magee

Journal Writing Question

Write your response to the question below.
Be ready to share your response.

What events could have occurred during the "lost year"?

Maniac Magee

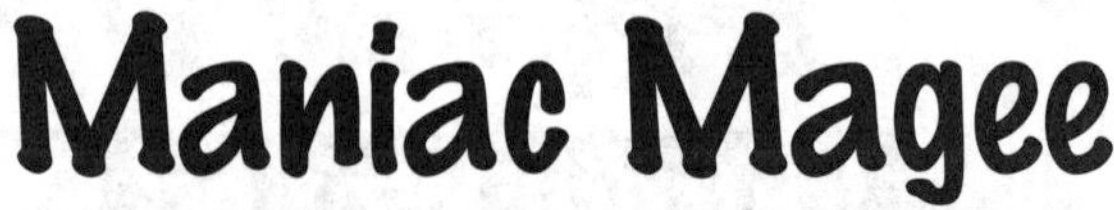
Question Starters

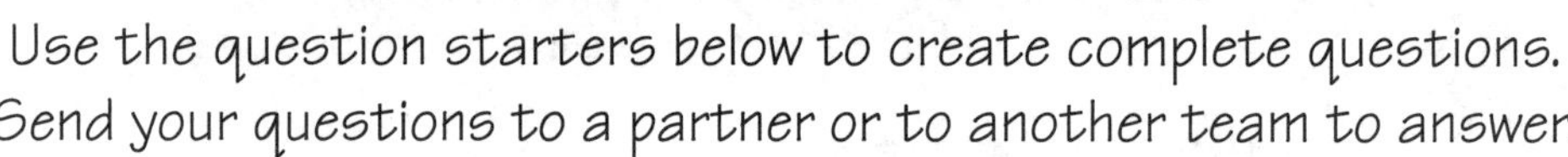
Use the question starters below to create complete questions.
Send your questions to a partner or to another team to answer.

1. Do you agree or disagree

2. What would others think of you if

3. How could you summarize

4. What part of the story

5. How was the conflict

6. What differences

7. What will happen

8. If you were Maniac

Higher-Level Thinking Questions for Intermediate Literature
Kagan Publishing • 1 (800) 933-2667 • www.KaganOnline.com

Missing May

higher-level thinking questions

Education is not the filling of a pail, but the lighting of a fire.

— William Butler Yeats

Missing May
Question Cards

Missing May
Question Cards

5 Cletus and Summer had an unusual relationship. Why are they so important to each other?

6 What things could Summer have done to help Ob recover from May's death? How helpful can children be to adults?

7 When they return from the Putnam County trip, how will Summer's and Cletus's friendship be different?

8 What does the old Chevy mean to Ob? Why has he kept it?

Higher-Level Thinking Questions for Intermediate Literature
Kagan Publishing • 1 (800) 933-2667 • www.KaganOnline.com

Missing May
Question Cards

Missing May

9 Ob's whirligigs are "art work." What do you think his whirligigs named "Fire," "Love," "Dreams," and "Death" looked like?

Missing May

10 Why is seeing the state capital so important to Cletus/Summer/Ob?

Missing May

11 How are the strengths of the characters different? What does this allow them to do for each other?

Missing May

12 How do you think Summer defines the word "home"? What is Cletus's definition? If they are different, why?

Missing May
Question Cards

Missing May

13 If you could choose Summer or Cletus for a friend, which would you pick? What qualities make you prefer her or him?

Missing May

14 If you created a whirligig for May's garden what would you call it? What would it look like?

Missing May

15 If Summer had kept a diary, what would she have put in it about her fears?

Missing May

16 Ob takes Cletus on the trip to Putnam County. In the next year what can Cletus do for Summer and Ob?

Higher-Level Thinking Questions for Intermediate Literature
Kagan Publishing • 1 (800) 933-2667 • www.KaganOnline.com

Missing May

Journal Writing Question

If Summer had kept a diary, what would she have put in it about her fears?

Missing May

Question Starters

Use the question starters below to create complete questions.
Send your questions to a partner or to another team to answer.

1. Would you be scared if

2. How would you describe the relationship between

3. If someone you loved died

4. How is your family

5. What part of the book

6. Does the setting

7. Is the conflict

8. What similarities

Higher-Level Thinking Questions for Intermediate Literature
Kagan Publishing • 1 (800) 933-2667 • www.KaganOnline.com

Mouse and the Motorcylce

higher-level thinking questions

Nothing pains some people more than having to think.

— Martin Luther King, Jr.

Mouse and the Motorcycle
Question Cards

Mouse and the Motorcycle

1 Describe your ultimate vacation.

Mouse and the Motorcycle

2 How would life be different if you were as small as a mouse?

Mouse and the Motorcycle

3 Do you think it is right to place yourself in danger to get what you really want?

Mouse and the Motorcycle

4 Why do you think Ralph, Keith, and Matt can all talk to each other?

Mouse and the Motorcycle
Question Cards

Mouse and the Motorcycle

5 If you were going on a trip what four items would you bring and why?

Mouse and the Motorcycle

6 Describe an exciting adventure you've had or would like to have.

Mouse and the Motorcycle

7 If you could order any meal, like Ralph did, what would it be?

Mouse and the Motorcycle

8 How is Ralph like another famous mouse in another story you've read?

Higher-Level Thinking Questions for Intermediate Literature
Kagan Publishing • 1 (800) 933-2667 • www.KaganOnline.com

Mouse and the Motorcycle
Question Cards

Mouse and the Motorcycle

9 Describe Ralph 10 years later.

Mouse and the Motorcycle

10 How is Ralph's family like or different than yours?

Mouse and the Motorcycle

11 After reading this book, what advice would you give to the owner of a pet mouse?

Mouse and the Motorcycle

12 Think of a time you helped a friend. Describe how you felt.

Mouse and the Motorcycle
Question Cards

Mouse and the Motorcycle

13 What could a new title be for this book?

Mouse and the Motorcycle

14 What advice might the ants have for Ralph?

Mouse and the Motorcycle

15 What might Ralph have said to the dogs that were barking at him when he was in the laundry pile?

Mouse and the Motorcycle

16 If you could interview Ralph on the TV news, what one question would the public want answered?

Higher-Level Thinking Questions for Intermediate Literature
Kagan Publishing • 1 (800) 933-2667 • www.KaganOnline.com

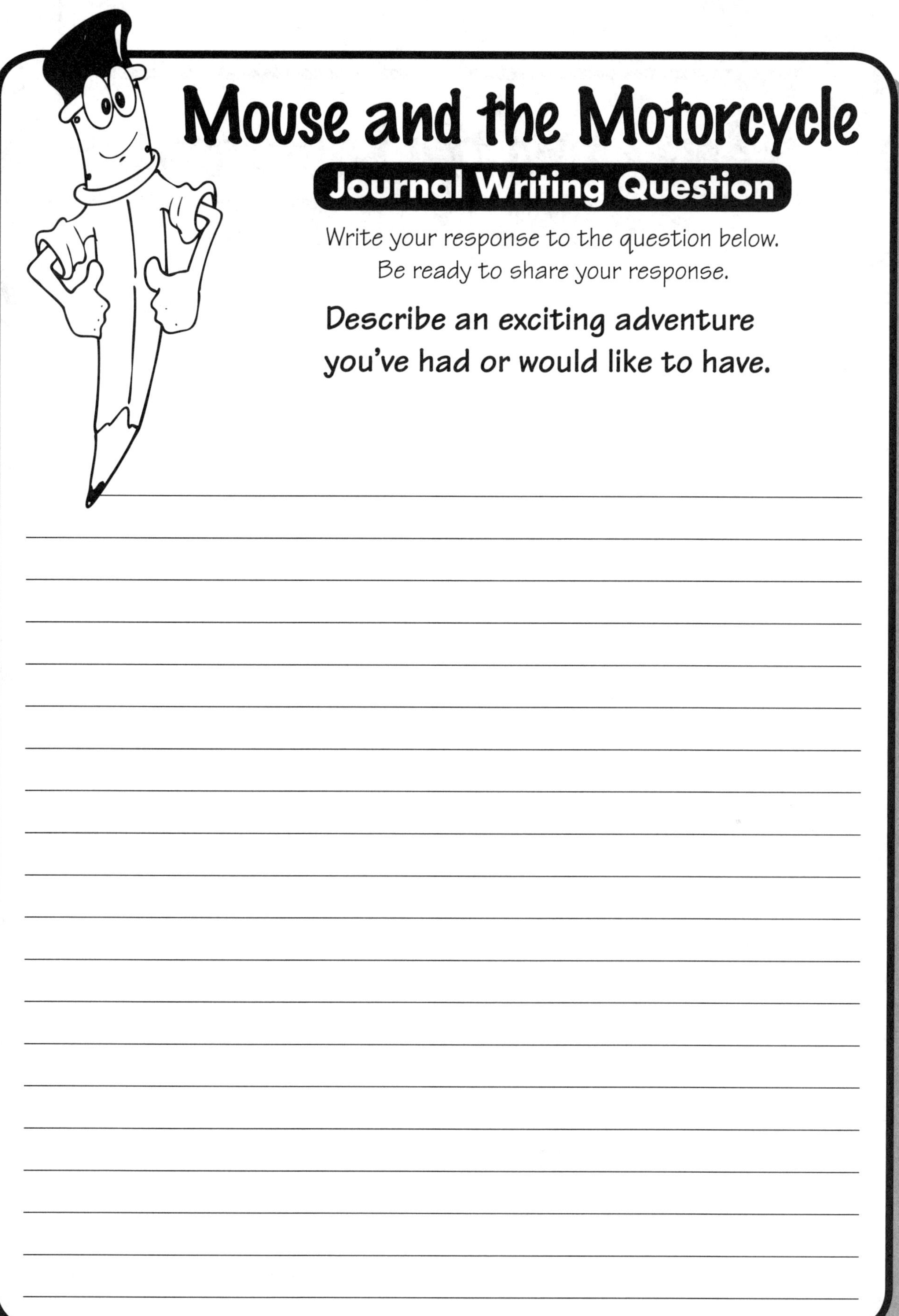

Mouse and the Motorcycle

Journal Writing Question

Write your response to the question below.
Be ready to share your response.

Describe an exciting adventure you've had or would like to have.

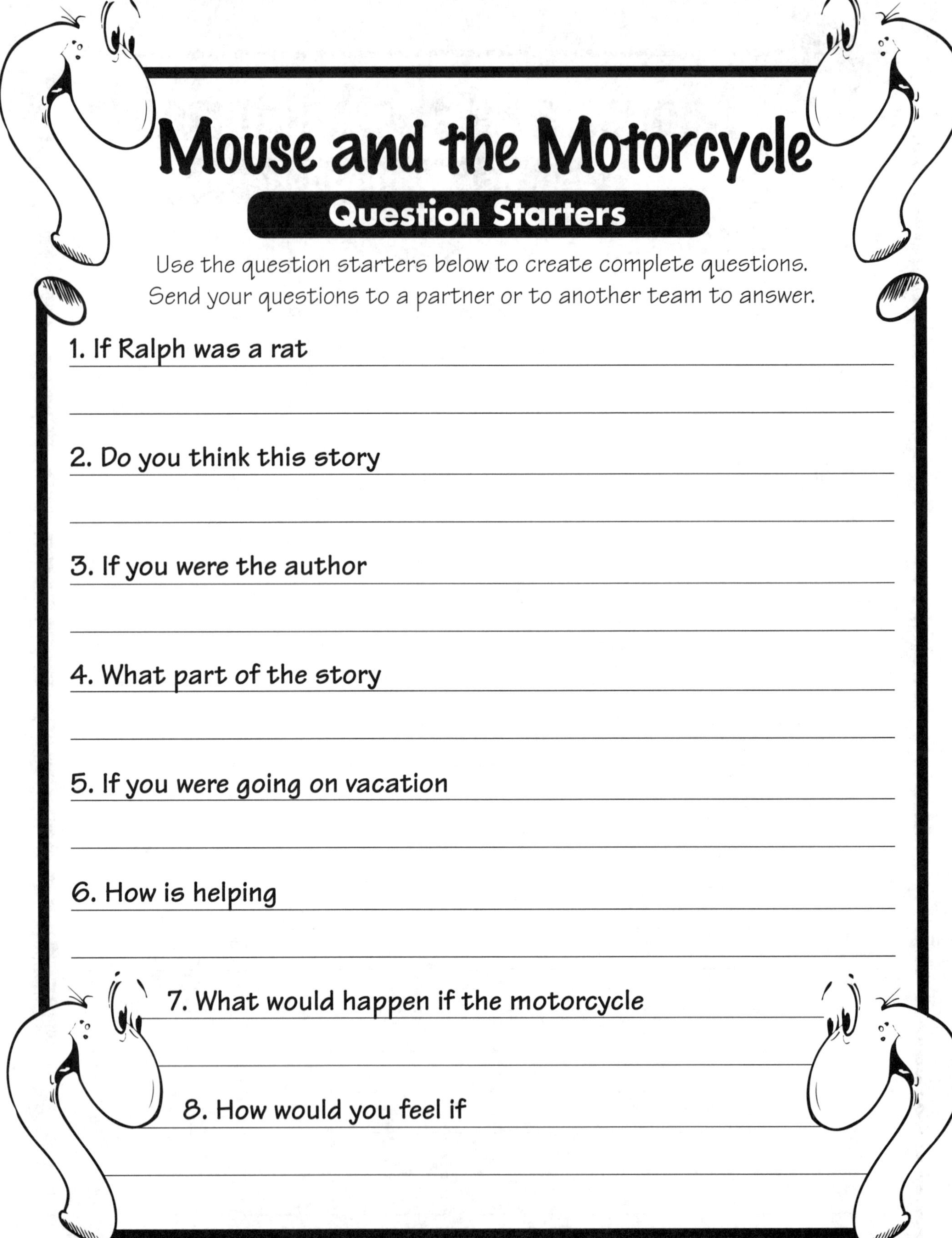

Mouse and the Motorcycle

Question Starters

Use the question starters below to create complete questions.
Send your questions to a partner or to another team to answer.

1. If Ralph was a rat

2. Do you think this story

3. If you were the author

4. What part of the story

5. If you were going on vacation

6. How is helping

7. What would happen if the motorcycle

8. How would you feel if

Higher-Level Thinking Questions for Intermediate Literature
Kagan Publishing • 1 (800) 933-2667 • www.KaganOnline.com

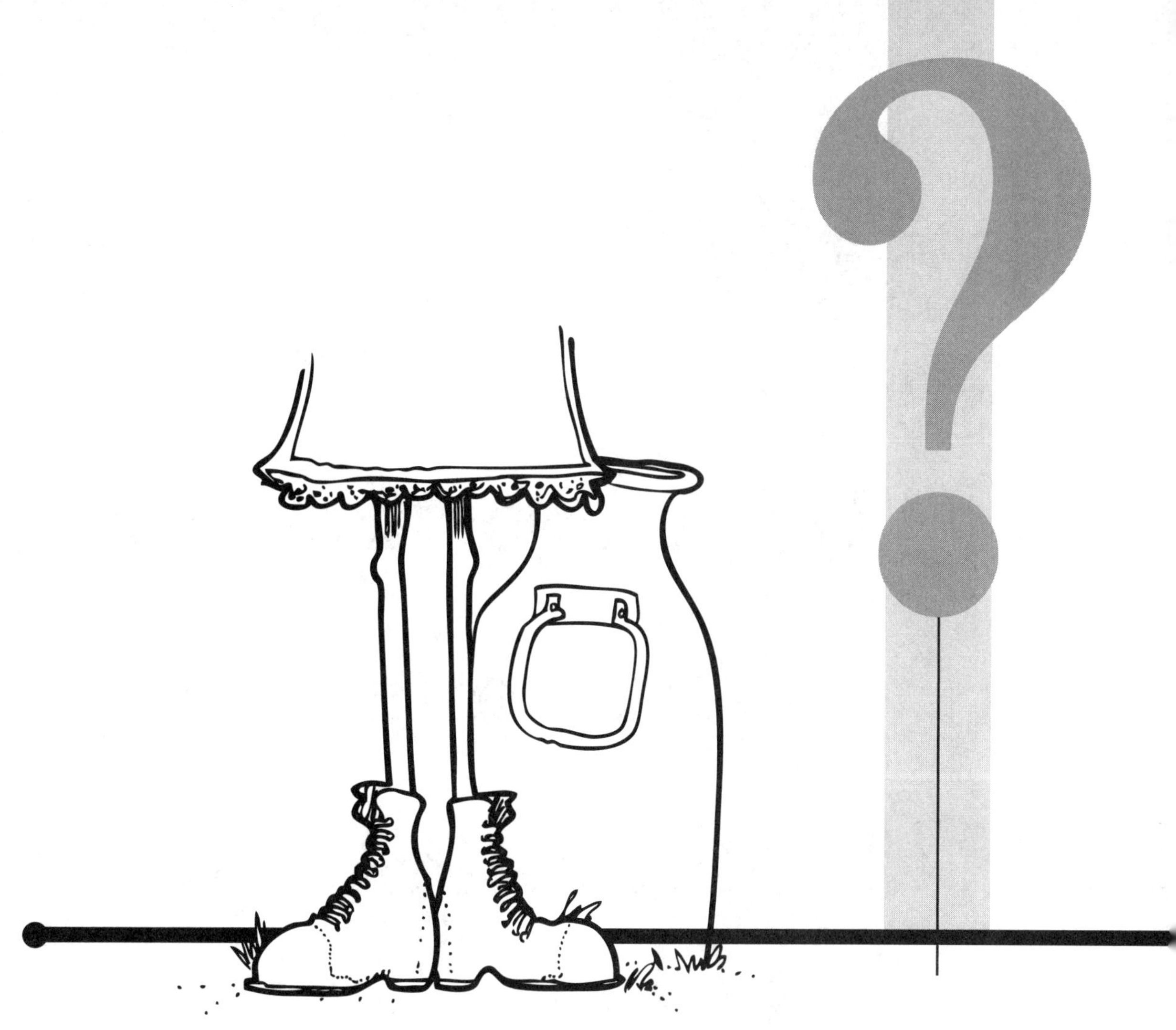

Sarah, Plain and Tall

higher-level thinking questions

The important thing is to never stop questioning.

— Albert Einstein

Sarah, Plain and Tall
Question Cards

1 What qualities does Sarah have that will make her a good mother for the children? What will make it difficult for Sarah to be their mother?

2 What is the biggest difference Sarah makes in each of the Wittings' lives? Explain your answer.

3 What could Anna and Caleb have done or said to make Sarah's decision easier to make?

4 When Sarah put on Jacob Witting's overalls, what new things did you learn about her?

Sarah, Plain and Tall
Question Cards

5 When Sarah writes to her brother, what will she tell him about the Wittings? What will she leave out of her letter?

6 The sea was important to Sarah. What is in your environment that is as important to you? Why is it important?

7 What reasons can you give for why Jacob Witting wrote his first letter to Sarah?

8 Why do you think Sarah brought her cat, Seal, with her on her visit?

Higher-Level Thinking Questions for Intermediate Literature
Kagan Publishing • 1 (800) 933-2667 • www.KaganOnline.com

Sarah, Plain and Tall
Question Cards

Sarah, Plain and Tall

9 If you were Sarah, what events would make you want to return home? Which people would make you want to stay?

Sarah, Plain and Tall

10 What could Jacob Witting have done to make Sarah want to stay and marry him?

Sarah, Plain and Tall

11 Why were Maggie's presents so important to Sarah? What presents would you have given Sarah?

Sarah, Plain and Tall

12 Sarah has a brother and Anna has a brother. How are these relationships the same? How are they different?

Sarah, Plain and Tall
Question Cards

13 If you were to write a letter to a person you had never met, what would you say about yourself?

14 If you were to draw a picture of your home or neighborhood, what parts would you want to be sure were colored?

15 If you were going to share songs with Anna and Caleb, what songs would they be?

16 If Sarah were to take the children to the sea coast, what ocean life would she want to be sure to share with them?

Higher-Level Thinking Questions for Intermediate Literature
Kagan Publishing • 1 (800) 933-2667 • www.KaganOnline.com

Sarah, Plain and Tall

Journal Writing Question

Write your response to the question below.
Be ready to share your response.

If you were to write a letter to a person you had never met, what would you say about yourself?

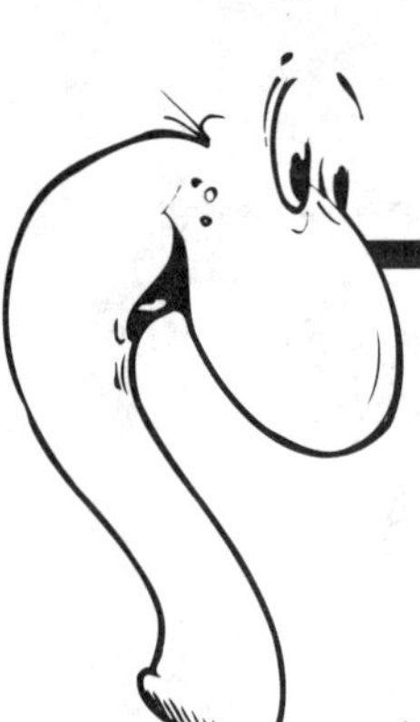

Sarah, Plain and Tall

Question Starters

Use the question starters below to create complete questions.
Send your questions to a partner or to another team to answer.

1. If you were Sarah

2. How are the Wittings

3. What would be different if

4. How would your life be different if

5. What could Sarah have said

6. Have you ever

7. How does the setting

8. How would your life be different if

Sign of the Beaver

higher-level thinking questions

**Teach the young people
how to think,
not what to think.**

— Sidney Sugarman

Sign of the Beaver
Question Cards

Sign of the Beaver

1 Which of your prized possessions would you be willing to give to a friend? Why?

Sign of the Beaver

2 Matt and Attean meet after a 20 year separation. Describe their conversation.

Sign of the Beaver

3 Create a new ending for the book.

Sign of the Beaver

4 What new character would you introduce to the story and why?

Sign of the Beaver
Question Cards

Sign of the Beaver

5 What might be the theme song for the movie version?

Sign of the Beaver

6 Share an important lesson you learned from a friend.

Sign of the Beaver

7 How will you know when you have become an adult?

Sign of the Beaver

8 Would you recommend this book to a friend? Why or why not?

Higher-Level Thinking Questions for Intermediate Literature
Kagan Publishing • 1 (800) 933-2667 • www.KaganOnline.com

<table>
<tr>
<td>

Sign of the Beaver

9 What skills might you develop while living in the wilderness?

</td>
<td>

Sign of the Beaver

10 What good things resulted from Ben's visit?

</td>
</tr>
<tr>
<td>

Sign of the Beaver

11 If Ben were arrested and tried for his crime, how might his lawyer defend him?

</td>
<td>

Sign of the Beaver

12 Choose one modern invention and explain how it might change the story.

</td>
</tr>
</table>

Sign of the Beaver
Question Cards

Sign of the Beaver

13 Imagine yourself alone in Matt's cabin for one month. What four items would you bring along?

Sign of the Beaver

14 How are Matt and Attean alike? How are they different?

Sign of the Beaver

15 Do you agree or disagree with Matt's decision to wait for his family? Why or why not?

Sign of the Beaver

16 Create a moral for the story.

Higher-Level Thinking Questions for Intermediate Literature
Kagan Publishing • 1 (800) 933-2667 • www.KaganOnline.com

Sign of the Beaver

Journal Writing Question

Write your response to the question below.
Be ready to share your response.

Matt and Attean meet after a 20 year separation. Describe their conversation.

Sign of the Beaver

Question Starters

Use the question starters below to create complete questions.
Send your questions to a partner or to another team to answer.

1. Why do you think Matt

2. Do you have a friend

3. What is the difference between

4. If the setting of the story changed

5. Why did the author make Ben

6. If you were Attean

7. What part of the story

8. Did the ending

Sylvester the Magic Pebble

higher-level thinking questions

Thought is, perhaps, the forerunner and even the mother of ideas, and ideas are the most powerful and the most useful things in the world.

— George Gardner

Sylvester the Magic Pebble
Question Cards

1 How is the magic pebble like or unlike magic in other stories you know?

2 Because of his adventure, how will Sylvester be different?

3 What advice do you think Sylvester's parents gave him when he returned home? What advice would you give Sylvester?

4 The magic pebble could be dangerous. When might it be all right to own something dangerous?

Sylvester the Magic Pebble
Question Cards

Sylvester the Magic Pebble

5 What would Mrs. Duncan have packed for their picnic lunch? What would you have packed?

Sylvester the Magic Pebble

6 What were some of the questions Sylvester asked his parents when he became himself again?

Sylvester the Magic Pebble

7 What might Sylvester use the pebble for after he is grown-up?

Sylvester the Magic Pebble

8 If you told your parents/friends that you had a magic pebble, what would they say?

Higher-Level Thinking Questions for Intermediate Literature
Kagan Publishing • 1 (800) 933-2667 • www.KaganOnline.com

Sylvester the Magic Pebble
Question Cards

Sylvester the Magic Pebble

9 Compare the magic pebble with magical objects in other stories. Which objects have the most powerful magic?

Sylvester the Magic Pebble

10 What will Sylvester's friends think about the magic pebble after Sylvester returns to his old self?

Sylvester the Magic Pebble

11 When Mr. Duncan tried to forget how sad he was about Sylvester what did he do to help himself? What do you do to try and forget something sad?

Sylvester the Magic Pebble

12 When Sylvester was a rock, what did he notice about the world around him? How did he adjust to his new situation?

Sylvester the Magic Pebble
Question Cards

13 How would the story have been different if Sylvester's hobby had been collecting buttons? Where could he have found a magic button?

14 How did the magic pebble come to be where Sylvester could find it?

15 If you found a magic pebble, what would you wish for yourself? What would you wish for others?

16 If the lion had found the pebble, what might he have wished for?

Higher-Level Thinking Questions for Intermediate Literature
Kagan Publishing • 1 (800) 933-2667 • www.KaganOnline.com

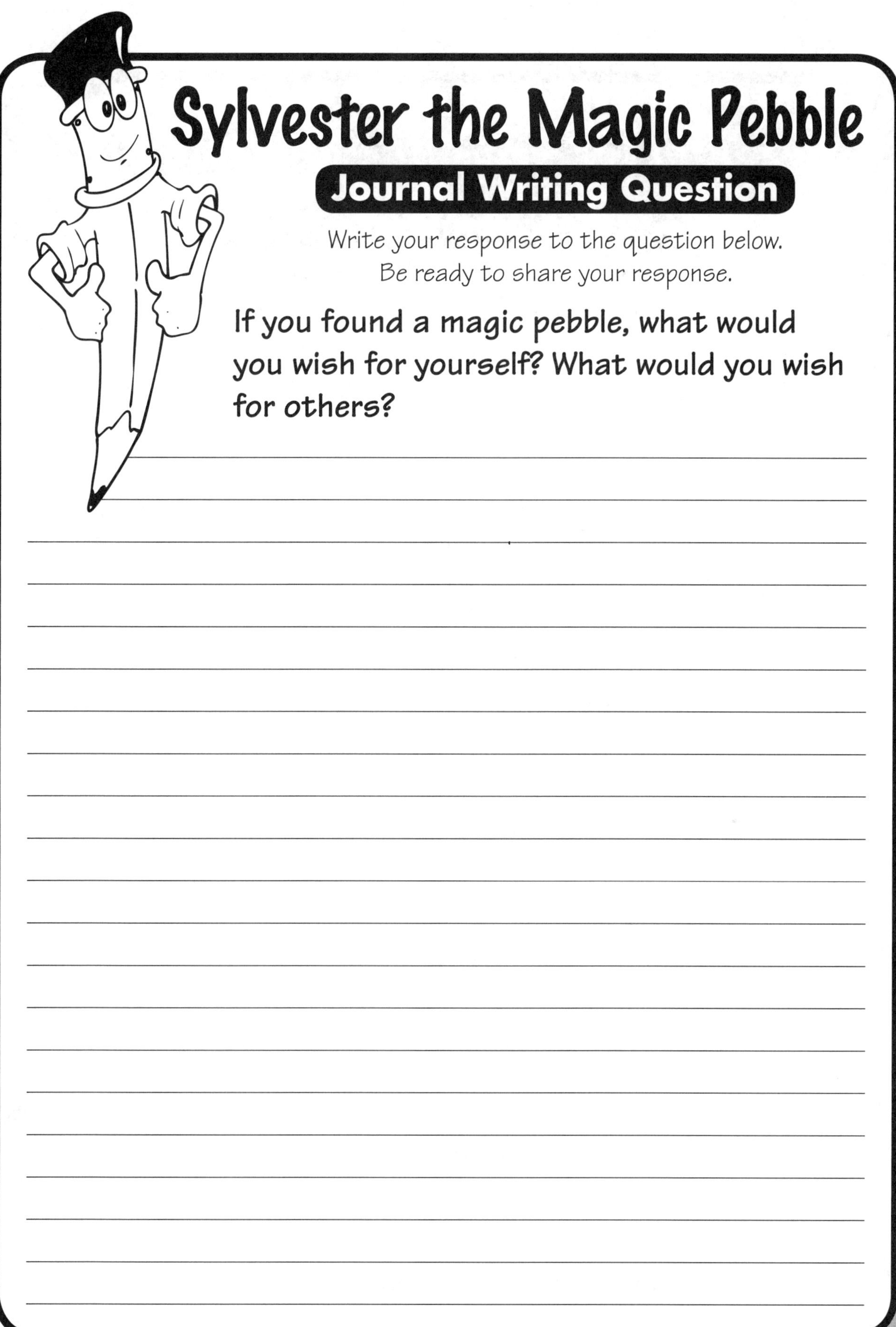

Sylvester the Magic Pebble
Journal Writing Question
Write your response to the question below.
Be ready to share your response.
If you found a magic pebble, what would you wish for yourself? What would you wish for others?

Sylvester the Magic Pebble

Question Starters

Use the question starters below to create complete questions.
Send your questions to a partner or to another team to answer.

1. If you found a magic pebble

2. How is the story like

3. Why did Sylvester

4. Would the plot change if

5. Would you recommend

6. What is another way

7. How do the characters

8. What part of the story

Higher-Level Thinking Questions for Intermediate Literature
Kagan Publishing • 1 (800) 933-2667 • www.KaganOnline.com

Notes

Question Books!

Light the Fires of Your Students' Minds with this Terrific Series of Higher-Level Thinking Question Books!

Promote Non-Stop Discussion

Sharpen Thinking Skills

Improve Writing Skills

Loaded with Hundreds of Provocative, Intriguing, Mind-Stretching Questions and Activities!

Call for Free Catalogs! Or Visit Us Online!

1 (800) 933-2667 *Kagan* www.KaganOnline.com

Kagan is the world leader

in creating active engagement in the classroom. Learn how to engage your students and you will boost achievement, prevent discipline problems, and make learning more fun and meaningful. Come join Kagan for a workshop or call Kagan to **set up a workshop for your school or district.** Experience the power of a Kagan workshop. **Experience the engagement!**

SPECIALIZING IN:

★ **Cooperative Learning**
★ **Win-Win Discipline**
★ **Brain-Friendly Teaching**
★ **Multiple Intelligences**
★ **Thinking Skills**
★ **Kagan Coaching**

KAGAN PROFESSIONAL DEVELOPMENT

www.KaganOnline.com ★ 1(800) 266-7576